Selection of Prague Hotels and Restaurants

Where do you start? Choosing a hotel or restaurant in an unfamiliar city can be daunting. It's even more bewildering in a place like Prague, with its inscrutable language and unaccustomed economic system. To help you find your way, we have selected a small but representative cross-section of the establishments that local sources recommend. We've taken into account the differing requirements of budget holidaymakers and businessmen, of conservative or adventurous travellers.

Our sample of hotels has been divided into three straightforward categories—high, medium and low price. The alphabetically-ordered restaurant list, however, is based on the type of establishment rather than the anticipated expense; in any case, most western visitors find most Prague restaurants reasonably priced if not downright cheap. Note that all the hotels named below have restaurants, some of them excellent. But we have confined our restaurant list to establishments beyond the hotel circuit.

Most of the year it's essential to have advance reservations at Prague hotels, for the city is seriously undersupplied with tourist accommodation. It's advisable, as well, to phone ahead for a table at any of the better restaurants. Unless otherwise specified, the listed restaurants and taverns are open daily.

HOTELS

HIGHER-PRICED

($110–$267 for double room with bath, breakfast included)

Hotel Alcron

Štěpánská 40
Prague 1
Tel. 245741
Telex 121814
143 rooms and suites
A few steps from Wenceslas Square. Traditional favourite of journalists and international businessmen. Garage.

Hotel Esplanade

Washingtonova 19
Prague 1
Tel. 226056-8
Telex 121067
63 rooms
Relatively small, stately hotel built in 1920s. Central location but quiet street. Highly regarded restaurant. Intimate nightclub.

Hotel Forum

Kongresová ul.
Prague 4
Tel. 410111
Telex 122100
531 rooms and suites
Skyscraper hotel across the road from Palace of Culture. All conveniences from satellite TV to business centre and fitness centre. Congress hall and conference hall.

Intercontinental Hotel

Náměstí Curieových
Prague 1
Tel. 2311812
Telex 122681
394 rooms and suites
Riverside location in centre of the city. Modern luxury-class accommodations, restaurants, nightclub with spectacular view of Prague Castle. Shopping. Business services. Underground garage.

Hotel Jalta

Václavské náměstí 45
Prague 1
Tel. 265541
Telex 121580
84 rooms and suites
1950s hotel facing Wenceslas Square. Restaurants, bars, nightclubs, terrace bar for fair-weather drinks on the square. Secretarial services.

MEDIUM-PRICED

($80–$110)

Hotel Ambassador

Václavské náměstí 5
Prague 1
Tel. 2143111
Telex 122137
114 rooms and suites
Facing Wenceslas Square. Restaurants (French style and Czech), bars, nightclub, terrace on the square.

3

Hotel International
Náměstí Družby 1
Prague 6
Tel. 339111
Telex 121055
257 rooms and suites
Prague's landmark Stalinesque skyscraper hotel, remote from central area. Grandiose halls. Garage.

Hotel Olympik
Sokolovská 138
Prague 8
Tel. 828541
Telex 121436
317 rooms and suites
Modern-style hotel, away from central Prague. Restaurants, bars, nightclub. Parking.

Hotel Panorama
Milevská 7
Prague 4
Tel. 416111
Telex 123576
432 rooms and suites
Vast modern hotel, distant from central district but on the Metro. "Relaxation centre" with swimming pool on 24th floor. Disco. Covered parking.

Parkhotel
Veletržní 20
Prague 7
Tel. 3897111
Telex 122278
234 rooms and suites
Modern-style hotel away from central Prague but accessible by Metro. Parking.

LOWER-PRICED
($45–$80)

Hotel Europa
Václavské náměstí 25
Prague 1
Tel. 263746
Telex 122103
110 rooms and suites
Well-preserved architectural landmark from 1906, facing Wenceslas Square. Splendid interior decor.

Hotel Paříž
U Obecního domu 1
Prague 1
Tel. 2322051
Telex 121082
86 rooms
In the centre of Prague, an architectural gem of neo-Gothic and fin de siècle styles. Enterprising restaurant.

Hotel Zlatá Husa
Václavské náměstí 7
Prague 1
Tel. 2143111
72 rooms
Alongside the Ambassador, an economical hotel with restaurants, wine cellar, video disco.

RESTAURANTS

Čínská restaurace
Vodičkova 19
Prague 1
Tel. 262697
*Expensive, surprisingly authentic
Chinese restaurant, mainly
Cantonese and Szechuan speciali-
ties. Reservation imperative.
Closed Sundays.*

Moskva
Na příkopě 29
Prague 1
Tel. 265821
*Flashy space-age decor. Russian
and Georgian specialities plus
do-it-yourself salad bar. Fast food
establishment downstairs.*

Obecní dům
Francouzská restaurace
Náměstí Republiky
Prague 1
Tel. 2318015
*Large ground-floor restaurant
with glittering art nouveau decor.
French and Czech cuisine.*

Opera Grill
Kar. Světlé
Prague 1
Tel. 265508
*Intimate restaurant with compre-
hensive menu, serving wine only
(no beer). Reservation essential.
Closed weekends.*

Pelikán
Na příkopě 7
Prague 1
Tel. 220781
*Upstairs in modern building a few
steps from Wenceslas Square.
Czech and international cuisine.*

Praha Expo 58
Letenské sady
Prague 7
Tel. 374546
*Known locally as "Brussels", it
introduced Czech food to the
World's Fair of 1958. Glassy
modern architecture overlooking
the river. Two restaurants, two
price levels.*

Valdštejnská hospoda
Valdštejnské náměstí 7
Prague 1
Tel. 536195
*In historic Lesser Quarter house
(a brewery was founded there
in 1352) alongside Wallenstein
Palace. Varied Czech and
international menu. Closed
Mondays.*

Vikárka
Vikářská 6
Prague 1
Tel. 535158
*Inside Prague Castle, facing the
north side of St. Vitus Cathedral.
Hearty Czech food and beer.
Open daily in summer, closed
Mondays in winter.*

WINE RESTAURANTS

Parnas
Smetanovo nábřeži 2
Prague 1
Tel. 265017
*Attached to famous Slavia café,
this elegant establishment enjoys a
view of river and castle. Where
local celebrities meet. Must book.*

Savarin
Na příkopě 10
Prague 1
Tel. 224778
*Sprawling through and around an
18th-century palace, a conglomer-
ation of restaurants, café, snack-
bar, garden, plus tea dancing.*

Sklípek Pana Broučka
Vikářská 6
Prague 1
Tel. 535158
*In an original Gothic cellar within
Prague Castle. Abundant meat,
fish, game, good wines. Open
daily in summer, closed Mondays
in winter.*

U Labutí
Hradčanské náměstí 11
Prague 1
Tel. 539476
*Just outside Prague Castle, "The
Swans" offers historic, intimate
atmosphere. Elegant cuisine and
gracious service. Must book.
Closed Sundays.*

U Lorety
Loretánské náměstí 8
Prague 1
Tel. 536025
*Alongside the convent (listen to
the famous chimes!). Outdoor
dining in season. Open daily in
summer, closed Mondays in
winter.*

U Malířů
Maltézské náměstí 11
Prague 1
Tel. 531883
*"The Painters", a typical old wine
restaurant in the Lesser Quarter,
long the hangout of artists. Closed
Sunday.*

U Mecenáše
Malostranské náměstí 10
Prague 1
Tel. 531883
*Medieval atmosphere – authentic
furniture, banners and pictures – in
a small Lesser Quarter restaurant
noted for good food at honest
prices. Closed Sundays.*

U Plebána
Betlémské náměstí 10
Prague 1
Tel. 265223
*Opposite Bethlehem Chapel, a
cool, intimate spot with Empire
style decor. Czech and foreign
(including Chinese!) food. Good
service. Closed Sundays.*

U Sedmi Andělů

Jilská 20
Prague 1
Tel. 266355
*"Seven Angels" occupies the
ground floor of a recently
renovated Gothic house near
Old Town Square.
Intimate atmosphere.*

U Zelené Žáby

U radnice 8
Prague 1
Tel. 262815
*Around the corner from
Old Town Hall, 15th-century
"Green Frog" specializes in
Bohemian wines. Closed Fridays,
Saturdays.*

U Zlatého Jelena

Celetná 11
Prague 1
Tel. 268595
*"Golden Stag" wine restaurant
in an elegant cellar
in historic "King's road"
pedestrian street.*

Viola

Národní 7
Prague 1
Tel. 235 8779
*Near the National Theatre, a
wine restaurant with offbeat
entertainment. Next door, the
Viola Trattoria, a small,
Italian-style bistro. Closed
Sundays.*

TAVERNS AND PUBS

U Dvou Koček

Uhelný trh 10
Prague 1
Tel. 267729
*In a quiet square near Bethlehem
Chapel, "Two Cats" is a crowded
pub with tasty food, good beer
and cheerful service.*

U Fleků

Křemencova 11
Prague 1
Tel. 292436
*Big but usually crowded, historic
pub features strong dark beer,
brewed on the premises. Hearty
local food. Music.*

U Kalicha

Na Bojišti 12
Prague 2
Tel. 296017
*The "Good Soldier Švejk" pub,
redolent of the old malingerer's
lifestyle. Fast-flowing beer and
Czech food enough to feed a
hungry army.*

U Medvídků

Na Perštýně 7
Prague 1
Tel. 235 8904
*Lively 15th-century pub, "The
Little Bears" features traditional
Czech cuisine and plenty of cold
beer. Closed Sundays.*

U Pinkasů
Jungmannovo náměstí 15
Prague 1
Tel. 261804
*Next to the unfinished complex of
the Church of Our Lady of the
Snows, this pub boasts a vast
turnover of Pilsner-Urquell 12°
beer.*

U Schnellů
Tomášská 2
Prague 1
Tel. 533218
*Rebuilt in 1787, this Lesser
Quarter tavern was a favourite
hangout of the operetta composer
Rudolf Friml, among others.*

U Supa
Celetná 22
Prague 1
Tel. 223042

*They've been drinking beer,
especially very strong lager, in
this popular pub since the 14th
century, but the inspiration for the
name–"the Vulture"—is obscure.*

U Sv. Tomáše
Letenská 12
Prague 1
Tel. 530064
*Outstanding medieval atmosphere
in this Lesser Quarter tavern
honouring St. Thomas, site of a
14th century brewery founded by
Augustinian monks.*

U Zlatého tygra
Husova 17
Prague 1
Tel. 265219
*The "Golden Tiger" has been a
beer cellar since the 13th century,
and the boisterous fun continues
daily except Sundays.*

BERLITZ®

PRAGUE

1991/1992 Edition

By the staff of Berlitz Guides

Berlitz Trademark Reg. U.S. Patent Office
and other countries – Marca Registrada.
Library of Congress Catalog Card
No. 88-72149.

Printed in Switzerland by Weber S.A.,
Bienne.

3rd Printing
1991/1992 Edition
_____ 1990

How to use our guide

- All the practical information, hints and tips that you will need before and during the trip start on page 105.
- For general background, see the sections Prague and its People, p.6, and A Brief History, p.14.
- All the sights to see are listed between pages 26 and 91. Our own choice of sights most highly recommended is pinpointed by the Berlitz traveller symbol.
- Entertainment, nightlife and other leisure activities are described between pages 91 and 97, while information on restaurants and cuisine is to be found on pages 98 to 104.
- Finally there is an index at the back of the book, pp.127–128.

Although we make every effort to ensure the accuracy of all the information in this book, changes occur incessantly. We cannot therefore take responsibility for facts, prices, addresses and circumstances in general that are constantly subject to alteration. Our guides are updated on a regular basis as we reprint, and we are always grateful to readers who let us know of any errors, changes or serious omissions they come across.

Photography: Claude Huber; pp. 6–7, 40 Čedok/Karel Vlček; pp. 13, 22, 25, 58, 75, 84, 90 Čedok/Bohumil Landisch; p. 94 Čedok/Daniel Sitenský
Layout: Doris Haldemann
We are particularly grateful to the staff of Čedok for their help in the preparation of this book.
Cartography: Falk Falk-Verlag, Hamburg.

Contents

Maps

Cover picture: Riverside scene in Prague

Prague and its People

For a thousand years the architects of Prague have used every artifice ever invented to embellish a building, from Gothic arcades to Renaissance windows to Rococo angels and Art Nouveau sylphs. The locals take the resulting spectacle in their stride, but this unparalleled panorama of beautiful history may just bowl you over.

Long before the "city of a hundred spires" acquired its uplifting skyline, the setting itself was inspiring. Picture the clear, wide Vltava River thrust-

ing through the ancient settlement, with forested hills on every horizon. It all began to develop in the 14th century under a great king, who made history not only as the local potentate but as ruler of the Holy Roman Empire.

Charles IV, a cultivated monarch, ordered a glorious urban development programme, including a bridge that became more than just a way to get to the other side of the river. For five centuries it was Prague's only span across the Vltava.

Bridges old and new straddle the city's ancient lifeline, the Vltava.

Now there are bridges up and down the river, but the Charles Bridge is still in use, and still indispensable. It's probably the prettiest bridge you'll ever walk across, or happily linger upon.

Prague's rich heritage attracts crowds of painters, photographers, architecture students and ordinary tourists who, in spite of everything they've heard and read, never fail to be surprised. Prague is even better than its publicity. Every detail—every tower and turret, pillar and portal—excels.

This overendowment of monuments might have gone up in smoke but for Prague's streak of luck in Europe's recent wars. While World War II bombing raids smashed the historic hearts of many other Central European cities, Prague was largely spared. When the dust had settled, the Czechoslovakian government invested a fortune in renovation. The avid conservation programme continues unabated.

But Prague offers much more than expensively maintained castles and art relics. As a city of 1.2 million, it's a political, commercial and, above all, cultural capital that lives, breathes, and even enjoys itself.

Take the pulse of Prague at the crossroads of the modern city, Wenceslas Square, named after Prince Wenceslas I, who reigned here a thousand years ago. (The Christmas carol which upgraded him to "Good King Wenceslas" is a fanciful 19th-century postscript.) Mingle with the crowd: proud parents pushing regal prams, well-dressed women window-shopping, provincial conscripts on leave gawking at the big city, briefcase-burdened bureaucrats, Third World students and Soviet tourist groups. Join the queue for an ice-cream cone, or for entry to a shoe shop. The patient people of Prague never shove or argue while they wait; they have nothing to learn from the English when it comes to disciplined queueing.

Equipped with old-fashioned manners, young people tend to give up their bus seats to the elderly. The young generation is taller, better looking and better dressed than ever. A few will go on to be film stars or tennis stars. Thousands will go on to university. Prague has a dozen institutions of higher learning (Einstein used to teach

No flourish was too extravagant for builders of beautiful Prague.

here). Charles University was founded in 1348, a century after University College, Oxford, making it Central Europe's oldest university.

You'll soon get your bearings in Prague. The ancient Prague Castle complex dominates the skyline, the tranquil Lesser Quarter in its shadow. The fortified castle, once the seat of the kings of Bohemia, still rules; it's the headquarters of the president of Czechoslovakia as well as an engrossing tourist attraction. Cross the bridge to the Gothic, Renaissance and baroque landmarks of the Old Town, and, nearby, the New Town (a mere six centuries old).

On the way from castle to museum to historic church, stop at an outdoor café and watch the scene unfold. Or drop into a traditional beer cellar or wine bar, so much a part of the capital's character. The greatest advertisement for Prague taverns was the Good Soldier Švejk, the supreme malingerer of World War I. In a triumph of passive resistance, the likeable Švejk managed to bamboozle every official who ever persecuted him. His Rabelaisian saga of the "little man" muddling through has inspired generations of Czechs. Like his creator, the Prague author

Jaroslav Hašek, Švejk tended to spend his evenings, and sometimes the whole day, in the city's congenial taverns.

If you had to point to Prague (*Praha* in Czech) on a map of Europe you might well miss the mark, for it's farther north and west than most people imagine. The city is even more northerly than Winnipeg, although the climate is milder, and farther west than Vienna. In the heart of Central Europe, on the political borderline between east and west, Prague is only 312 kilometres (194 miles) by motorway from Vienna and 347 kilometres (215 miles) from Berlin.

The city's area is a generous 497 square kilometres (192 square miles), about two-thirds the size of the vastly more populous New York City. This leaves space for Prague's extensive parks, forests and sports grounds, and an outstanding zoo where the animals have enough room to roam.

Central Prague, though, is as congested with cars as any other big city. Aggravating the problem, road space is restricted by the priorities of pedestrian zones and construction or reconstruction projects. (At any time perhaps one in five of all the old buildings in Prague seems to be hidden behind scaffolding; the work goes on listlessly for years, by which time newer edifices are old enough to need restoring.) And new buildings are going up in all the suburbs—endless housing projects to ease the shortage of apartments.

Notwithstanding Prague's rather westerly location on the map, 20th-century history assigned it to the eastern bloc for more than four decades. The red flags and pro-proletarian slogans were swept away by the "velvet revolution" of 1989. But other relics of the communist era are slower to disappear. Take the Comecon-style traffic jams, featuring local Škodas, East German Trabants, Soviet-produced Ladas and Volgas, and a few ceremonious Tatras. The smoggy scene is almost as exotic as rush hour in Moscow.

Other communist achievements will linger longer than Stalin statues: highways, highrises and sports facilities. But the most admirable of these is Prague's clean, efficient Metro, the underground rail service that almost any city in the world could envy. At last report a ticket cost perhaps one-tenth what it would in the west.

Visible or not, the changes in Czechoslovakia are almost tangibly exciting. This is a rare chance to witness history in the making.

If getting around is cheap, fast and easy, that's no reason to rush. This is a walking town, where every corner you turn may reveal a new delight. Some of Prague's most memorable features can only be appreciated from up close: a street-corner shrine, a proudly sagging roof, a stately lamp post, a cubist window.

Sightseeing out of town, through forests, orchards and fields of hops, the order of the day is castles. In Czechoslovakia, a country of 2,500 castles, the highlight sights are these fortified retreats of the old nobility, perched in commanding locations. Organized day-trips from Prague give you a choice of half a dozen important castles, each different. The closest, 14th-century Karlštejn, was reinforced by the Habsburgs; Konopiště, a Gothic castle transformed into a hunting lodge, is filled with Archduke Franz Ferdinand's hunting trophies. Another popular excursion features the spa of Karlovy Vary (known to Bach, Goethe and Peter the Great as Karlsbad), with a stop on the way at the tragically evocative town of Lidice.

After a spate of sightseeing

A mouthful of Karlsbad's water, an eyeful of medieval Prague.

Prague offers relaxation on many levels. The theatre is festive and bargain-priced—see Shakespeare in Czech, or **12** a mime show, or the famous *Laterna Magika* multi-media spectacle. Music has always been a good bet here, whether it be really grand opera, a concert by the Czech Philharmonic Orchestra, or contemporary excitements. (Prague is where *Don Giovanni* had its premiere, Beethoven and Liszt performed, and the composers

Smetana, Dvořák and Janáček made their names.)

Or you can have dinner to the accompaniment of a brass band—a meal as old-fashioned as the tunes; forget *nouvelle cuisine* and dig into roast pork with cabbage immersed in a gravy that's substantial enough to float the dumplings.

(Dumplings, which come in bread or potato variants, are all but inevitable in Czechoslovakia.) Afterwards, you may wind up in a boisterous cabaret, a noisy nightclub, or a quiet bar where the fruit brandy goes down as effortlessly as the sun setting over Golden Prague.

13

A Brief History

The long, often violent history of Prague reads like the fever chart of a hospital patient in seesaw condition, a dramatic zigzag of ups and downs. In eras when favour frowned, the troughs were deep and long, but in good times, Prague has been truly great.

Figures as distinguished as Good King Wenceslas, Holy Roman Emperor Charles IV, Jan Hus and the Habsburg family drop in and out of the often lurid narrative, which flows as vividly as spilled blood.

For thousands of years travellers have been interested in the site of Prague, for it is a natural fording place on the Vltava River, which is linked with the Elbe. Details of these earliest arrivals are disclosed in locally excavated Stone Age vestiges, from tools to jewels.

Celtic tribesmen settled in the area well over two thousand years ago, followed by a Germanic people. Of more

Czechoslovakia in Perspective

Geography: Landlocked in Central Europe, Czechoslovakia is bordered by Poland, East Germany, West Germany, Austria, Hungary and the USSR. Its area is 127,889 square kilometres (49,365 square miles)—about the same as New York state, or one-fourth the size of Spain. Highest point: Gerlach Peak in the High Tatras, 2,655 metres (8,711 feet) above sea level.

Population: About 15.5 million. Czechs outnumber Slovaks by about two to one.

Government: Federation of Czech and Slovak republics. Multiparty system replaces more than 40 years of communist rule.

Industry: Formerly geared to Comecon economics, Czechoslovakia's industries include power engineering, metallurgy, automobiles, glass, leather and chemicals. Agriculture produces grains, sugar beets, potatoes.

Religion: Most churches in Czechoslovakia are Roman Catholic.

Languages: Czech and Slovak, related and mutually comprehensible Slavic tongues.

lasting significance, the first Slavs—ancestors of the Czechs—arrived in the 5th or 6th century A.D., choosing hilltops for safety more than the view.

In the second half of the 9th century, the original fortifications of the castle were built. From here the Czechs were ruled by members of the Přemyslid family, a dynasty going back to mythical roots and forward well into the Middle Ages.

A Saintly Pioneer

A Greek preacher named Methodius is credited with bringing Christianity to the Slavs late in the 9th century. The erudite itinerant set an example for the ordinary citizens when he baptized Prince Bořivoj. Methodius went on to be declared a saint. So, separately, did Bořivoj's widow, Ludmilla. This devoutly Christian lady was assassinated, the victim of a pagan cabal. Many a royal murder was to follow, but the steadfast Ludmilla was assured her place as patron saint of Bohemia.

The grandson of Ludmilla, the first of the rulers named Wenceslas (*Václav* in Czech), held the stage relatively briefly in the 10th century. During his reign a church dedicated to St. Vitus was built at Prague Castle. Wenceslas, a fervent believer, became the first of the Czech princes to be murdered on the job—actually, he was ambushed on his way to mass. It was a family affair in the classic pattern, a compound of jealousy, religious disagreement and political greed. The killer was his younger brother, Boleslav.

Far from being condemned for eliminating the saintly Wenceslas, Boleslav took power and held it for nearly half a century. During his reign a well-travelled Arab merchant wrote admiringly of Prague as a busy trading centre with solid buildings of stone. The town became the seat of a bishop in 973.

Early in the 11th century Boleslav's great-grandson, Břetislav I, extended Přemyslid rule to neighbouring Moravia. He went on to become a vassal of the German emperor, opening the door to centuries of German influence. Bretislav's son, Vratislav II, was the first monarch to bear the title of King of Bohemia. Hundreds of years later other Europeans began using the word Bohemian to mean gypsy, referring by extension to spiritedly unconventional, perhaps irresponsible, people, such as artists. "Bohemian" is not the word that would come to mind today to describe a typical citizen of Prague.

More Wenceslases

Among kings, namesakes are about as common as jesters, but the Wenceslas saga is exceptionally confusing. Prince Wenceslas I, the saint, was not the only Wenceslas I. The second Wenceslas I became King of Bohemia in 1230, and ruled long and well. He encouraged the arts, and presided over a growing prosperity—and population. Since the beginning of the 13th century, immigrants from Germany had been moving into Bohemia. Some of them settled in Prague. In 1257, King Otakar II founded the Lesser Quarter as a German enclave, protected by German law.

Wenceslas II, Otakar's son, was notable for his diplomatic skills. However, there was nothing very diplomatic about the way he dealt with a threat to his power from his opportunistic stepfather; Wenceslas had the old man executed. Thanks to big silver finds at this time the economy went from strength to strength, and the Prague *groschen* became a stable international currency.

Luck, and the dynasty, ran out with the son of Wences-las II. In the summer of 1306, early in his reign, the teenaged king was assassinated in Moravia. The killer was never found. Wenceslas III went down in history as the last of the Přemyslid kings.

The Great Charles

Another Wenceslas grew up to be the king who transformed Prague from a provincial town into an important world capital. As a young man, getting a good education in Paris, this prince chose to become an ex-Wenceslas, changing his name to a more pronounceable Charles.

He was the son of John of Luxembourg, a man of action who ruled Bohemia for 36 years. Wenceslas/Charles gave his name for France, but his francophile father gave his life. King John was killed in 1346, early in the Hundred Years' War, fighting on the losing side at the Battle of Crécy.

Even before his coronation the future Charles IV was deeply involved in running Prague and Bohemia. His relations with the church were always warm, and in 1344 he convinced the pope to promote Prague to an archbishopric. Under his direction centuries of work began on the present St. Vitus Cathedral, the glorious

Inside Prague Castle: one facet of majestic St. Vitus Cathedral.

Gothic centrepiece of Hradčany Castle. Early in his reign Charles acted to put Prague firmly on the intellectual map of the world. He founded central Europe's first university. He expanded the city to the New Town, providing room for useful immigrants from all of Europe—craftsmen, merchants and artists. Prague became the world's fourth biggest city in area. Not far from town he built Karlštejn Castle, to keep the crown jewels out of harm's way. Finally, he gave Prague its Gothic bridge, the Charles Bridge, still a useful and beautiful link between the Old Town and Lesser Quarter.

In 1355 Charles added a historic crown to his regalia when he went to Rome for his coronation as Holy Roman Emperor. Back in Prague he ruled nobly over the empire, as well as Bohemia, until his death in 1378.

Religious Strife

The city of Prague should have thrived as the administrative headquarters of the empire Charlemagne started, but people and events conspired against it. Charles IV's son and successor, named Wenceslas IV, turned out to be the wrong man for the job. He might have proved adequate in quieter times, but his reign was marred by feuds, revolts and wars. An irresolute leader, Wenceslas turned his back on distant problems, and even ignored some crises in Prague itself. The Holy Roman Empire deposed him. On the home front, he was the target of a couple of palace coups.

In the most momentous crisis that Wenceslas failed to address, Prague lived through the first skirmishes of a prelude to the Reformation. At Prague's Bethlehem Chapel a priest, theologian and professor named Jan Hus challenged the excess-prone Catholic church of the day to change its ways. Hus's demands for reform became so vigorous that he was excommunicated, then arrested for heresy, and finally burned at the stake in 1415. Czech nationalists and religious reformers far beyond Prague never forgot him. Wenceslas IV, who started out as a lukewarm supporter of reform, failed to save Hus's life.

The movement went marching on with ever wider popular support, to the dismay of the Vatican. In 1419 a reformist mob invaded Prague's New

3-D effects adorn a Renaissance palace facing Hradčany Square.

Town Hall, liberated imprisoned Hussites, and threw several Catholic city councillors from the windows. History calls this event the First Defenestration of Prague. It was the start of a long tradition. In Prague, throwing out officials could mean throwing them out the window, literally.

The harried brother of the unfortunate Wenceslas, King Sigismund, marshalled the Czech Catholic forces and foreign allies in a crusade against the Hussites. But the rebels fought back. Their underequipped but highly motivated peasant army won some famous victories, defeating Sigismund at the Battle of Vítkov Hill and other foes far afield. The rebels were commanded by a brilliant one-eyed soldier, Jan Žižka, who invented a new kind of warfare, improvising a mobile artillery force on primitively armoured farm wagons. In spite of the success of his roving cannonry it was another two centuries before conventional armies followed Žižka's lead. Eventually, inevitably, the rebels were defeated, but their saga is richly remembered today in Czechoslovakia.

The monarchy entered a crisis when Sigismund died without leaving a clear successor. His son-in-law, Albrecht of Austria, was thrust into the gap but soon died. Awkwardly, Albrecht's only son was born after his father's death; he was known by the unfortunate title of Ladislas Posthumous. Though his claim to the throne was successful, the lad's career was cut short. Rumours long persisted that poor Posthumous had been murdered, though a recent investigation suggested natural causes. The alleged poisoner was George of Poděbrady, a dynamic politician who, in spite of the bad publicity, was elected to succeed him.

George sided with the Hussites, to the growing displeasure of the neighbouring Catholic kings and a couple of popes in a row. He ended up excommunicated and boycotted, which wasn't good for Prague's business. Although a rival king disputed his throne, George refused to quit. He died, peacefully, in office.

Four Habsburg Centuries

Absentee kings absent-mindedly ruled Bohemia from George's death until 1526, when the Habsburgs claimed the throne. But even these serious monarchs were too busy with their responsibilities elsewhere in the Holy Roman Empire—for instance, fighting off the galloping advance of the Turkish army—to accomplish much in Prague. Mostly they tried to cope with Bohemia's grave religious divisions. By now the Protestant faith had become a powerful influence; but the Habsburgs were zealous Catholics.

The nicest thing the eccentric Rudolph II did for Bohemia was to move his capital from Vienna to Prague. Under this imperial impulse the arts and sciences reached new heights, and splendid Renaissance buildings further beautified the city. The emperor, centuries ahead of his time, was psychologically disturbed. This encouraged his political opponents to whittle away at his authority. The main accomplishment of his reign (1576–1612) was a decree granting freedom of religion to Catholics and Protestants alike. However the Catholic king, Ferdinand II, did not honour it. This exacerbated the religious conflict which soon escalated into the suffering of the Thirty Years' War.

One of the first incidents in the violent struggle was another of those Prague defenestrations. This time the window was in the Bohemian Chancellery of Prague Castle, and the victims were a couple of governors and their secretary, all accused of anti-Protestant actions. They bounced back from the experience with curable injuries.

In the ensuing rebellion Ferdinand was deposed, but his supporters rallied and, with a lot of help from elsewhere in the empire, triumphed in the Battle of the White Mountain, fought on Prague's doorstep. Restored to power, Ferdinand sent a convincing message about loyalty to the populace: he had a couple of dozen rebel leaders executed in the Old Town Square. Eliminating, as well, any theological subtleties, Roman Catholicism was proclaimed the only legal religion.

Ferdinand's decisive victory radically changed the face of Prague, haggard as it was after the fighting and stripped of its role as imperial capital. The majority of Protestant landowners emigrated to more welcoming climes, their property going to Ferdinand's Catholic supporters. Those who stayed behind were forced to convert to Catholicism, and many ordinary citizens converted as well. Baroque architecture of the sort favoured in Catholic Italy became the fashion. The medieval atmosphere of Prague gave way to the extravagances of 17th-century palaces and a parade of baroque churches advertizing **21**

Pointing out the date on Prague's celebrated old astronomical clock.

the triumph of the Counter-Reformation.

From this time forward, German, not Czech, tended to be spoken in palace and court-house. The tensions that grew up between Prague's German- and Czech-speaking citizens would persist well into the 20th century.

Maria Theresa & Son

Only one queen ever reigned over Prague. Maria Theresa had impressive credentials as the daughter, wife and mother of Holy Roman emperors. Between diplomatic engagements she produced 16 children, including the future Queen Marie-Antoinette of France. Prague's citizens were fertile, as well: during her long rule the population grew to more than 80,000. This was the era of the Seven Years' War. (The wars were getting shorter but no less fierce.) In the Battle of Prague, in 1757, the Prussian King Frederick the Great beat the defenders but withdrew when other battlefronts called. At one stage the situation was so difficult that Maria Theresa had to pawn the family jewels.

Under her son and heir, Joseph II, religious toleration was restored. Joseph also abolished serfdom and relaxed censorship. On the municipal level, he created a consolidated city of Prague from its four components—Hradčany, Lesser Quarter, Old Town and New Town. Music provides a gauge of the cultural development of Joseph's Prague: in 1787 Mozart was invited to conduct the world première of *Don Giovanni* in the theatre now named the Tyl. It was a hit, though critics in Vienna later panned the opera. Mozart always appreciated Prague's good taste.

Industrial Prague

By the second third of the 19th century Prague's population had topped 100,000. Factories were built and a railway line opened between Vienna and Prague, signalling the Industrial Revolution. Bohemia went on to become the most advanced manufacturing centre of the Austrian Empire.

Another kind of revolution broke out in 1848, uniting Czech nationalists and the new working class of Prague against the overlords in Vienna; communist historians called it the bourgeois revolution. The remote, rigid Austrian authorities soon extinguished the uprising, but not the smouldering nationalist feelings of the Czechs. When Prague's monumental National Theatre opened in 1881 the first work performed was a new opera by Smetana, a patriotic saga called *Libuše*. Dvořák, too, took inspiration from Czech folk songs. Nationalist Prague was conspicuously out of step with the rhythm of the capital, Vienna, the home of the waltz.

The 20th Century

When the heir to the Habsburg throne, Archduke Franz Ferdinand, was assassinated in 1914, the far-flung Austro-Hungarian Empire was plunged into the carnage of World War I. Prague was put under a state of emergency and its young men were shipped off to fight for the Kaiser in Czech-speaking units. Meanwhile, the Bolshevik Revolution in Russia sent ripples to Prague and beyond, though the Communist Party of Czechoslovakia wasn't founded until 1921. **23**

From the ashes of the defeated Austria-Hungary an independent Czechoslovakian republic was proclaimed in October 1918. Prague was the capital of the First Republic, comprising Bohemia, Moravia and Slovakia. The first president was Tomáš G. Masaryk, a widely travelled and admired philosophy professor. Re-elected three times, he died in retirement in 1937, before the agony of yet another European war.

Czechoslovakia was at the vortex of the storm that blew up into World War II. In September 1938, six months after the annexation of Austria, Hitler demanded self-determination for Czechoslovakia's German-speaking citizens. To appease him, Britain and France handed over the country's western provinces to the Third Reich at a great powers conference in Munich. Czechoslovakia was further diminished when Poland and Hungary rushed in with territorial claims of their own. Then Hitler threatened to rain bombs on Prague unless the remains of the country were made a German protectorate. The government of what remained of Czechoslovakia's Second Republic capitulated. Six years of occupation ensued.

The New Czechoslovakia

In May 1945, the resistance forces in Prague led an insurrection against the Germans. The rebels held out for four days until Soviet troops liberated the capital, opening a new era. When parliamentary elections were held a year later, the communists won nearly 40 per cent of the votes. The non-communist pre-war president Edvard Beneš, elected again, invited the veteran communist leader Klement Gottwald to form a coalition cabinet.

Gottwald, who had spent the war years in the Soviet Union, seized his big chance in 1948. When non-communist ministers resigned in protest against his one-sided policies, Gottwald packed the government. Beneš, saying he did it to avoid bloodshed, bowed to the power play. But he refused to sign a new constitution the communists steamrollered through parliament, and resigned. (Beneš , who had suffered two strokes, soon died of natural causes, a few months after his defenestrated foreign minister, Jan Masaryk; whether Masaryk jumped or was pushed has never been proved.)

Gottwald, as president, framed a five-year economic plan, cracked down on the churches, and purged his opponents outside and then inside the party. Scores of political figures were executed, thousands arrested. Gottwald died suddenly in 1953, a few days after attending the funeral of his mentor, Stalin. Under Antonin Novotn'y the show trials went on. Farmers were forced into collectives and the arts were smothered under the rules of Socialist Realism.

Long after the Soviets desanctified Stalin, the Prague party line conceded that Gottwald, too, had cultivated a personality cult. His famous victims were posthumously honoured as sincere communists. (In Prague, cynics said anybody can predict the future; only the past is unpredictable.)

A reform movement in the late 1960s culminated in the "Prague Spring" under Alexander Dubček, the head of the Slovak communist party. Unshackling the press and the arts, Dubček promised "socialism with a human face". But this was 20 years before its time. On August 20, 1968, reform was crushed by the armed forces of the Soviet Union, assisted by East Germany, Poland, Hungary and Bulgaria, ostensibly by invitation. As the world watched Soviet tanks rumbling through Wenceslas square, Prague wept.

The nation's leading intellectuals fled to the west or were relegated to menial jobs; Dubček wound up an unmentionable "un-person", effectively under house arrest. The new party chiefs turned, with limited success, to economic development, maintaining hardline traditions even when the winds of change blew in from Moscow.

In 1989, Wenceslas Square was again the scene of repression: television showed the police clubbing peaceful students who demonstrated for an end to one-party rule. But this time the long-suffering citizens had had enough. Now Prague's seemingly invincible communist regime, all alone in a fast-changing Europe, cringed before the voice of the people raised in outrage. When hundreds of thousands of protestors marched on Prague Castle, the police waved them through. Playwright Vaclav Havel called it the "velvet revolution".

Dubček, rehabilitated, was elected chairman of a rejuvenated parliament. And Havel, an ex-dissident freshly out of jail, was sentenced to a term in the castle—as the nation's president by acclamation. It was a scenario even a dramatist wouldn't have dreamed up. **25**

What to See

Since the days of Charles IV Prague has been the sum of four main parts, each with its distinctive character. Two elements of the equation are found on each side of the ever-present Vltava River. The most monumental portion, on the heights overlooking the rest of the city, is Hradčany, the ancient district featuring Prague Castle. Beneath it, the charming Lesser Quarter (Malá Strana in Czech, literally meaning Small Side) was established in the 13th century. Across the river, the Old Town (Staré Město) is one of Europe's best-preserved medieval capitals, including remarkable vestiges of the Jewish ghetto.

Follow the Signs	
hrad	castle
kaple	chapel
kostel	church
klášter	convent, monastery
město	town, city
most	bridge
muzeum	museum
nábřeží	embankment
náměstí	square
palác	palace
památník	monument
ulice	street
věž	tower
zahrada	garden

Next to the Old Town, the (relatively) New Town (Nové Město) is rich in parks and gardens, Gothic and baroque architecture. (Prague's baroque buildings have enough caryatids to hold up a medium-sized town all by themselves.)

You can get a notion of Prague's geography and character on a guided coach tour, but then you should switch to the most gratifying sightseeing plan: exploring the city, neighbourhood by neighbourhood, on foot. After you've tackled the highlights, try to squeeze in an excursion or two to the Bohemian countryside and its grand castles.

Castle District

From across the river, Prague Castle looks like a sweeping cliff crowned with palaces, topped in unequivocal glory by the spires of a great cathedral. A thousand years ago, the bulwarks were of mud and the church was a primitive round chapel. But one thing about the fortress hasn't changed. As it was in the age of Prague's first prince, the castle remains the home base of the country's

Cityscape in the Castle District inspires an artist and onlookers.

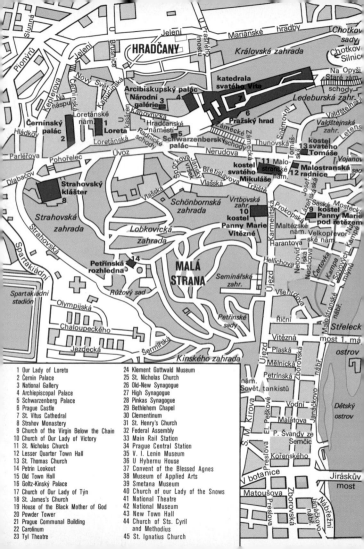

1 Our Lady of Loreto
2 Černín Palace
3 National Gallery
4 Archiepiscopal Palace
5 Schwarzenberg Palace
6 Prague Castle
7 St. Vitus Cathedral
8 Strahov Monastery
9 Church of the Virgin Below the Chain
10 Church of Our Lady of Victory
11 St. Nicholas Church
12 Lesser Quarter Town Hall
13 St. Thomas Church
14 Petrin Lookout
15 Old Town Hall
16 Goltz-Kinský Palace
17 Church of Our Lady of Týn
18 St. James's Church
19 House of the Black Mother of God
20 Powder Tower
21 Prague Communal Building
22 Carolinum
23 Tyl Theatre
24 Klement Gottwald Museum
25 St. Nicholas Church
26 Old-New Synagogue
27 High Synagogue
28 Pinkas Synagogue
29 Bethlehem Chapel
30 Clementinum
31 St. Henry's Church
32 Federal Assembly
33 Main Rail Station
34 Prague Central Station
35 V. I. Lenin Museum
36 U Hybernu House
37 Convent of the Blessed Agnes
38 Museum of Applied Arts
39 Smetana Museum
40 Church of our Lady of the Snows
41 National Theatre
42 National Museum
43 New Town Hall
44 Church of Sts. Cyril and Methodius
45 St. Ignatius Church

Letenské sady

Na ovčíně

nábř. kpt. Jaroše

Svermův most

Vltava →

200   400 m

200   400 yard

M = Metro station

nábř. Ludvíka Svobody

Na Františku

Anežský
klaster   37

STARÉ

MĚSTO

Staronová
synagóga

Vysoké
synagóga

Mašťálské
nám.

Dlouhá

uměleckoprůmyslové
muzeum   38

Pinkasova
synagóga   28

Starý žid.
hřbitově

kostel
svatého
Mikuláše   16

palác
Goltz-Kinských

Staroměst-
ské nám.   17

kostel
svatého
Jakuba

Obecní
dům   36

U hybernú
dům

nádraží
Praha
střed   34

Staroměstská
radnice
a Orloj

kostel
Panny Marie
pod Týnem   19

Celetná
dům u černé
Matky boží   23

Prašná
brána   20

muzeum
V. I.
Lenina   35

Klementinum   30

Karolinum

Tylovo
divadlo

Muzeum
Klementa
Gottwalda   24

nám. M.
Gorkého
kostel
svatého
Jindřicha

Betlémská
kaple   29

Uhelný
trh

Hlavní
33 nádraží

chrám Panny
Marie Sněžné   40

NOVÉ MĚSTO

Národní
divadlo

Federální
shromáždění

Riegrovy
sady

Novoměstská
radnice   43

Národní
muzeum   42

kostel svatého
Cyril a Metoděje   44

Malá
Štěpánská

45 kostel
svátého
Ignáce

CENTRAL PRAGUE

political chieftain, now titled the President of the Czech and Slovak Federative Republic.

You can enter the castle compound from three directions—north, east or west. Excursion parties normally approach from the west, proceed on foot through the enclave and depart, an hour or two later, through the eastern ramparts. In the next several pages of our What to See section we follow the same general itinerary. Walking from west to east here has an advantage: it's all downhill.

A soaring clock tower—its Dutch-made carillon of 27 bells plays an hourly hymn—introduces one of Prague's most impressive baroque structures, a shrine called simply **Loreta** (Our Lady of Loreto). On the edge of Prague Castle, this elaborate set of cloisters is fronted by a stately 18th-century façade.

At the centre of a grassy courtyard rather cluttered with statuary is the "santa casa", a representation of the house in which, according to tradition, the Virgin Mary was born in Nazareth. Angels were said to have carried it to the Italian town of Loreto, now a major shrine. This is one of dozens of copies of the house that were built in Bohemia to rally the peasants to the Counter-Ref-

ormation. Another attraction inside Loreta is the Church of the Nativity *(kostel Narození Páně)*, a small, lavishly decorated 18th-century church.

The **treasury**, upstairs in the cloister, glitters with precious reliquaries, monstrances and mitres, well displayed with captions in English, French and German as well as Czech. Pride of place goes to a monstrance from Vienna, dated 1699, encrusted with thousands of diamonds—in fact, enough sparklers to light a cathedral.

Černin Palace *(Černínský palác)*, across the wide square from the Loreta, has a monumental baroque façade extending for 150 metres (nearly 500 feet). Built by a noble diplomat in the 17th century, the palace was recruited as a barracks in the middle of the 19th century. Now restored to its old elegance, the palace serves modern diplomacy as Czechoslovakia's Ministry of Foreign Affairs.

Hradčany Square

An irregularly shaped medieval town square, Hradčanské náměstí, leads to the entrance of Prague Castle. Although the centuries have changed its face, the place is still full of historical flourishes. Notice the baroque **plague column**, erected by the grateful survivors of an epidemic in the early 18th century. Earlier, the less lucky leaders of a 1547 uprising were executed here for failing to overthrow King Ferdinand I.

The **Tuscan Palace** *(Toskánský palác)* on the west side of the square, is typical of the splendour of late 17th-century baroque. The coats of arms of the Dukes of Tuscany, who used to own the building, can still be seen on the façade.

The former **Martinic Palace** *(Martinický palác)* was built in the early 17th century in Renaissance style. The exterior decorations feature *sgraffito* ("scratched" plaster) illustra-

tions of mythological and biblical stories. Generally the square's palaces are used either as museums or offices; this one is the office of the city architect, who ought to be inspired by the view.

The **Archiepiscopal Palace** *(Arcibiskupský palác)* has been through several stages of development, most significantly the late 17th-century baroque aspect, to which Rococo details were added. The public has one chance per year to view its exuberant interior, on the Thursday before Easter. Behind the archbishop's palace, the former Sternberg Palace *(Šternberský palác)*, houses the praiseworthy

European art collection of the **National Gallery***.

Finally, have a look at the former **Schwarzenberg Palace** *(Schwarzenberský palác)*, a Renaissance triumph from the middle of the 16th century. The windows on each floor are a different shape, and the façade is decorated with *sgraffito* effects simulating rows of facets spiking from the walls. Restored after World War II, the palace now contains Prague's **Military Museum,** covering 5,000 years of military history.

👜 Prague Castle

A castle may mean a fortress or a Disneyesque turreted building or a walled complex of contiguous, often fanciful structures. Prague Castle *(Pražský hrad)* is a city in itself, in the manner of Moscow's Kremlin or Granada's Alhambra, though several centuries older than either of them. Any way you go about it, seeing Prague Castle, with its array of churches, palaces, towers and museums, involves a lot of walking.

Facing Hradčany Square, the ceremonial entrance to this encyclopaedia of history and architecture is guarded by a couple of white-gloved army

sentries standing at attention on either side of the main gate. Above them, outsized statues of mythological giants are shown using dagger and bludgeon, respectively, to despatch their foes. Don't let them put you off.

Once through the gate you're in the First Courtyard *(první*

*For a description of Prague's museums, refer to the chapter beginning on page 72.

nádvoří) of the castle, an 18th-century afterthought. As you walk on through the **Matthias Gate** *(Matyášova brána)*, a baroque triumphal arch, look to your right; the glass doors lead to the headquarters of the Czechoslovakian president.

The Second Courtyard *(druhé nádvoří)*, built over an an-

Menacing mythological sentries guard Castle's outer courtyard.

cient moat, is much bigger and older than the first. In the north-west corner is a small modern museum, the **Prague Castle Picture Gallery**, stocked with a selection of old masters. **33**

Before it went highbrow this part of the castle was a stable. To the south the **Holy Cross Chapel** *(kaple svatého Kříže)* now contains objects from the treasury of St. Vitus Cathedral, including a coat of mail said to have belonged to Good King Wenceslas.

In the biggest enclave, the **Third Courtyard** *(třetí nádvoří)*, stands the greatest sight of all: **St. Vitus Cathedral** *(katedrála svatého Víta)*. Its majestic western façade calls to mind Notre-Dame in Paris, but the truth is that this part is 19th-century neo-Gothic. For Prague's biggest church was a thousand years abuilding.

The original church on this site was ordered by Prince Wenceslas in the early 10th century, well before he was promoted to saint. The present building began in the reign of the enterprising Emperor Charles IV. The first of generations of architects involved was a 14th-century Frenchman, Matthias of Arras, who was succeeded by Peter Parler, a prolific German architect and sculptor, and his two sons. The whole project was finally completed in 1929.

The cathedral's **south façade** is decorated with hundreds of years of inspiring art. Over the porch is a much-restored 14th-

century mosaic of the *Last Judgement,* including contemporary portraits of Charles IV and one of his queens, Elizabeth of Pomerania. (All four of Charles's wives are buried together here.) Let your eye wander left and upwards to the gold-filigreed Renaissance grillework in a Gothic window. Above is a pair of single-handed clocks, the upper one indicating the hour and the lower, the quarter-hour. Complementing all these features is the delicate tracery, as light and intricate as leaves on a tree.

Inside the cathedral, the most beautiful of the many chapels is dedicated to St. Wenceslas. Peter Parler designed and adorned it in the middle of the 14th century, some 400 years after the young prince's murder. Nearer the high altar, there's a stairway from the Holy Cross Chapel to the burial vault, where you can see the tombs of some of the most distinguished royal personages, as well as parts of the original 10th-century Romanesque church. Otherwise, there's much to admire as you explore the cathedral, from the Gothic oratory to the Renaissance pulpit to the 20th-century stained glass windows.

Just north of the cathedral, the **Powder Tower** *(Mihulka)* was part of the castle's 15th-century defences. Restored in modern times, the circular tower has become a small museum. The ground floor covers the military aspects of the tower, with an exhibit of Renaissance science and technology upstairs. In the basement an exposition of metal casting recalls the 16th century, when this tower was used as a foundry.

The **Royal Palace** *(Královský palác)* is the secular equivalent of the cathedral—a medieval striving for grandeur in stone. It was the home of the kings of Bohemia until the 16th century, when the Habsburgs turned it into offices and warehouses.

The palace's **Vladislav Hall** *(Vladislavský sál)*, regal in design and dimensions, was be-

Cathedral treasures are devoutly displayed in Holy Cross Chapel.

gun in 1493. The architect, Benedikt Ried, was knighted for his achievement. It's called the largest secular hall built in the late Middle Ages. Tournaments were held here, with as many as 100 horsemen involved; today's tourists depart down the staircase designed for the horses. The hall's intertwining ribbon vaults, 13 metres (43 feet) high, add grace to the pompous setting. Imagine a throng of subjects arrayed here to pay homage to their king, or for a plenary meeting of the lords.

For a couple of hundred years the province of Bohemia was governed from the **Bohemian Chancellery** *(Česká kancelář)*, just off Vladislav Hall. In the second, smaller room, the citizens refined the concept of the window of opportunity. History was made here with a

In Prague's prime panorama, the Cathedral rises over the Castle.

splash in 1618 when two governors and their clerk were defenestrated (see p. 21). As you'll notice, it's a long way down, but they survived.

Diagonally across the vast Vladislav Hall, the former **Hall of the Diet** *(Stará sněmovna)* exudes medieval dignity. The supreme court used to sit here —note the paintings of Habsburg kings on the walls.

Founded in the early years of the 10th century, **St. George's Basilica** *(bazilika svatého Jiří)*

is considered Prague's oldest surviving church. Sighting its ochre baroque façade, facing St. George's Square, you'd never guess there's a fetchingly restored Romanesque church inside. It features the tombs of Prince Vratislav, the founder of the church, and of Boleslav II (known as Boleslav the Pious). The 13th-century wall-paintings are Prague's oldest. Next door the former Convent of St. George *(Jiřský klášter)* also dates from the 10th century. Czechoslovakia's first convent was dissolved in 1782 by Emperor Joseph II. Now belonging to the National Gallery, it contains the matchless **Collection of Old Bohemian Art**.

A final "must-see" attraction in the castle: **Golden Lane** *(Zlatá ulička)* is a narrow cul-de-sac (dead-end street) with pastel houses that photographers find irresistible; you'll be uncommonly lucky to get a picture that doesn't show a herd of other photographers in the foreground. In the 16th century these tiny houses, built into the ramparts, were occupied by archers defending the castle. Later assorted artisans lived and worked here, among them goldsmiths (hence the name of the street). Now most of the houses are souvenir shops. 37

Strahov Monastery

Amidst tall trees on the hill south-west of the Castle district sprawls the architectural complex of the Strahov Monastery *(Strahovský klášter),* founded in 1140. The original wooden building, put up for the just-organized Premonstratensian order, was soon replaced by a more substantial Romanesque structure. At the time it was even more elaborate than the castle itself. But it burned down. The monastery's Gothic and Renaissance successors finally gave way to an all-embracing baroque facelift. Some precious early aspects have been preserved.

Apart from two baroque churches (one now converted to an exhibition hall) the monastery is remarkable for its lavish **library**. Hundreds of thousands of books are only part of the story here: the vaulted ceilings and stucco ornament overwhelm. There are, in fact, two collections of books, one devoted to philosophy and the other to theology. Now both form part of the **National Literature Museum.** You'll wonder how scholars managed to climb the ladders up the two-storey bookcases in the Philosophical Hall, for the sight of the ceiling frescoes can be quite dizzying.

Lesser Quarter

For baroque charm, no area of Prague is such an unalloyed delight as the Lesser Quarter *(Malá Strana).* Rising, imperceptibly at first, from the riverside to Hradčany, this is the second oldest part of the city. The street plan dates from the middle of the 13th century, and the reign of Otakar II, who encouraged German immigrants to settle here. But Malá Strana rarely looks its age, as almost every monument of the early days was wiped out by a series of fires in the Middle Ages. Then the district was rebuilt in Renaissance and, subsequently, baroque style, with a stately but cosy appeal.

In this section, we begin to explore Malá Strana from the riverside, an attractive approach, especially when it means crossing the Vltava via Prague's most splendid bridge.

Charles Bridge

For the far-seeing Holy Roman Emperor, Charles IV, the bridge that now bears his name was a utilitarian project. In the 14th century the townsfolk simply needed a solid stone link

Charles Bridge: a span, a place to meet, and a sculpture gallery.

above flood level. In 1870 what had heretofore been called the Prague Bridge or the Stone Bridge was renamed, in his honour, the Charles Bridge *(Karlův most)*. By then the trusty Gothic structure had acquired the baroque adornments that make it an exhilarating work of art. Due to some complications during construction and reconstruction, the bridge isn't the shortest distance between two points; here and there its path veers slightly, as if the blueprints had become wrinkled. Although wide enough to carry modern motor traffic, it's reserved for pedestrians. Stroll across it at a leisurely pace, stopping now and then to admire the view from—and of—the bridge.

Starting from the east (Old Town) side of the river, the bridge is introduced by a Gothic **tower** massive enough to daunt almost any prospective invader. The architect and sculptor Peter Parler was responsible for this innovation, as well as the statues thereon of his sponsors, Charles IV and Wenceslas IV (seated), and the bridge's patron, St. Vitus.

Not quite arrow straight, Charles Bridge crosses to the Old Town. **41**

Altogether 30 **statues** or sculptural groups line the bridge, 15 on each side. Dating primarily from the 18th and 19th centuries (though a few are modern copies), each one has a history behind it. On the right side of the bridge, the Crucifixion scene includes a large 17th-century Hebrew inscription, paid for by a rich Jew accused of blasphemy. Midway across the bridge, the oldest statue, cast in bronze in 1683, honours a local martyr. St. John of Nepomuk was drowned at this spot three centuries earlier on the orders of King Wenceslas IV. It was long rumoured that the priest was executed for refusing to reveal the confessions of the king's wife. But Father John's actual offence was political: he sided with his archbishop in a dispute with the king.

Beyond, on the opposite side, an 18th-century statue movingly portrays St. Lutgard kissing the wounds of Christ. And the next-to-last sculptural ensemble on the left offers a terrifying view of captive Christians, guarded by a bored-looking Turkish jailer armed with a scimitar and barbed whip.

In some of the niches beneath the sculptures, modern artists sell their paintings and drawings of the bridge and the city—or propose an instant portrait of any passing patron of the arts.

Number, Please

Don't let the street numbers of Prague drive you up the wall.

Most buildings have two kinds of numbers prominently affixed. The blue plaque announces the normal street number; if you're looking for 24 Somewhere Street, you'll find it (in blue) next to number 22. But house 22 may also have a big red plaque reading "19", while house 24, next door, bears the red number "162". The red numbers, non-geographical, indicate the order in which the buildings entered the municipal register; the lower the number in red, the older the house.

The Left Bank

Guarding the western end of the bridge are two Gothic towers connected by an arch, the **Malá Strana Gate.** The ensemble was begun late in the 12th century. Here begins **Mostecká Street,** a narrow shopping street lined with fine baroque houses. It was part of the King's Road, the route of coronation processions. For a brief diversion, turn left into Lázeňská Street, leading to a quiet, distinguished neighbour-

hood. Peter the Great and Chateaubriand used to stay in the former hotel at No. 6, now a very gloomy place.

A Maltese cross marks the **Church of the Virgin Below the Chain** *(kostel Panny Marie pod řetězem)*, originally a 12th-century basilica which belonged to the Knights of Malta. The baroque palaces facing **Knights of Malta Square** *(Maltézské náměstí)* house a library, the **Museum of Musical Instruments,** the Japanese embassy and a cabaret.

You'd hardly know the low-lying district of **Kampa** was an island, but it's separated from the "mainland" of Malá

Orbs at the ready, Charles IV and St. Vitus guard the bridge.

Strana by a narrow arm of the Vltava once used to power watermills. Although no single building stands out, most of the baroque houses here contribute to an all-round air of dignity and good taste.

The atmosphere today in busy Karmelitská Street is a far, noisy cry from the contemplative scene chosen by the Carmelites for their convent. The **Church of Our Lady of Victory** *(kostel Panny Marie Vítězné)* was the city's first baroque building. Construction 43 began in 1611; it was a Protestant church until the barefoot Carmelites took it over a few years later. What draws coachloads of foreign tourists to this church is not the architecture but a Renaissance **statuette** of the "Holy Infant of Prague". It was brought to Prague from Spain in the mid-16th century.

Up the Hill

From many parts of Prague you can see an unlikely silhouette on the horizon—a copy of the Eiffel Tower. The local version is less than one-fourth the size of the original, but its site on Petřín Hill adds to its stature. The **Petřín Lookout** *(Petřínská rozhledna),* as it is called, was built for the Prague Industrial Exhibition of 1891, only two years after Gustav Eiffel's engineering exploit amazed Paris. Inevitably, in recent times it was commandeered as a television transmitting tower.

In the same area of parkland you'll find an astronomical observatory, three venerable churches and a relic of the 1891 fair—a maze built of mirrors.

A favourite way to reach Petřín Hill is by funicular *(lanová dráha* in Czech). To find the cable-propelled train's Malá Strana terminal, follow the red signs along Újezd Street.

Lesser Quarter Square

Strolling through the pedestrian zone of Prague Castle may have spoiled you for the main square of the Lesser Quarter, **Malostranské náměstí.** The pressure of traffic distracts from the flavour of its fine old arcaded buildings.

Looming over it all is the massive dome and bell tower of Prague's greatest baroque church, **St. Nicholas** *(kostel svatého Mikuláše).* The architect was the Bavarian Christoph Dientzenhofer; after his death at the age of 71 his talented son Kilian continued the project and improved it. This was a Jesuit church, designed to display the order's power after the success of the Counter-Reformation. But soon after it was finished the Jesuits were dissolved by Pope Clement XIV, so St. Nicholas was confiscated for use as a parish church. It remains so today.

The church's interior is a sumptuous anthology of religious art, topped by one of the biggest ceiling **frescoes** in Europe. The artist, Jan Lukáš Kracker, covered 1,500 square metres (nearly one-third of an acre) with scenes from the life of St. Nicholas. Notice, too, the fresco inside the cupola, by Francis Xavier Palko. Beneath the dome, surrounded by giant statues of saints, the crucial crucifix on the main altar is scarcely bigger than you'd find on the wall of a monk's cell, an effective contrast.

In the square in front of the church, an elaborate plague column is surrounded by haphazardly parked cars. Its construction was sponsored by the survivors of a 1715 epidemic. Behind the church, the other, much busier part of the square is lined with substantial buildings linked by an arcade— a good place to hide from a rain storm. Notable is the Late Renaissance **Lesser Quarter Town Hall** *(Malostranská radnice)*, an early 17th-century landmark on the site of the original 15th-century town hall.

St. Thomas Church *(kostel svatého Tomáše)*, around the corner, underwent a baroque facelift in the early 18th century. The younger Dientzenhofer takes credit. Peter Paul Rubens *cannot* take credit for the powerful paintings of St. Thomas and St. Augustine at the altar, which are copies. The originals are on display in Prague's National Gallery.

Letenská Street leads to the rear of Prague's most luxurious palace, and the way in to the **Wallenstein Garden** *(Valdštejnská zahrada)*, open to the public from May through September. These formal gardens, as big as a city park, were laid out in the early 17th century, an Italian baroque whim designed to impress the neighbours. It surely succeeded. The main avenue of the park is lined with statues. They are, in fact, copies; the 17th-century originals by the expatriate Dutch sculptor Adrian de Vries were hauled off to Sweden during the Thirty Years' War. The garden makes a delightful setting for summer plays and concerts. As for the palace, the work of Italian architects, the Ministry of Education currently enjoys its vastness.

The man who built the palace, Generalissimo Albrecht Wenzel Eusebius von Wallenstein, also known here as von Waldstein, came to an unhappy end. Although he had all the money imaginable, having married a rich Czech widow, and considerable political power, he decided to try for the throne of Bohemia. The incumbent emperor, Ferdinand II, frowned on Wallenstein's conspiracy and ordered his assassination; an English officer, Captain Walter Devereux, did the honours with a halberd. The German poet Schiller, 166 years later, chose the Wallenstein saga as the subject of his greatest play.

Old Town

From Prague's earliest days, its strategic importance in the centre of Europe has been evident to friend and foe. While power was barricaded in the castle on the hill, rough-and-ready commerce animated the opposite bank of the Vltava, at the junction of the traditional trading routes linking Europe's east, west, north and south. It was only a few centuries before the teeming market place evolved into a distinguished main square from which a jumble of historic streets radiate. Prague's Old Town *(Staré Město)* has more medieval delights and baroque surprises than you can take in at a single survey. Start at the ancient crossroads.

Hub of Old Town

In an irregular open space as vast as Red Square in Moscow, **Old Town Square** *(Staroměstské náměstí)* provides a dazzling panorama. Stand in the middle and turn a slow circle: it's as if all the most charming city streets of Europe were stretched around you. Vying for beautiful superlatives, every building is different in every detail—roof, windows, doors, and colours from the most unconventional, yet pleasing palette: tangerine and pistacchio, apple red and lime green. You can get your bearings in central Prague from two sets of towers overlooking this low-rise scene. The multi-turreted twin towers to the east belong to the Týn church, while the Gothic clock tower of the medieval town hall stands at the south-west corner.

If the architecture isn't enough to give you pause, consider the historic events which unfolded on these cobblestones: the demonstrations, the proclamations, the executions, the parades, triumphal or muted.

The urban panorama is interrupted to the north by a mighty **monument** to Jan Hus, teacher, preacher and martyr. It was officially dedicated in 1915 on the 500th anniversary of the reformer's flaming execution for heresy. The inscription reads, "Truth will prevail."

The **Old Town Hall** *(Staroměstská radnice)*, begun in the 14th century, has developed in slow bounds to match the municipality's growth in size and importance. Neighbouring houses were incorporated, and additions and modifications

Waiting for a wedding party at the magnificent Old Town Hall.

46

continued to be made until the 19th century, as if generations of "do-it-yourself" enthusiasts had established a tradition of expanding and improving the old family house. But the structure suffered badly during the last hours of World War II, and the east wing is still to be restored.

The most obvious highlight of the Old Town Hall is its 15th-century **astronomical clock**. Every hour on the hour, as crowds in the square look on, clockwork figures on the tower's façade enact a timely story: Death consults his hourglass and yanks a bell cord; Christ and the Apostles appear, and other characters swing into action. Finally, a cock crows. Below, an immensely complicated clock tells the time, tracks the movements of the sun and moon (assum-

For centuries, Týn Church spires have topped Old Town skyline.

ing, of course, that the earth is the centre of the universe), and displays the signs of the zodiac. The bottom dial indicates the months in pictures. After you've seen the spectacle, you can enter the building for a guided tour, which lasts less than half an hour. Highlights are the sumptuous **halls** with their 15th-century aura, intricate ceilings and murals and tapestries. Nowadays much of the town hall is used for exhibitions.

Abutting the town hall, on the left side, is one of Prague's most memorable Renaissance buildings. The five-storey **Dům U Minuty** (literally, House at the Minute) is emblazoned with *sgraffito* decorations on biblical and mythological themes. Overlooking the square from a corner niche of the house is an 18th-century stone lion.

On the north-east edge of the square, the former **Goltz-Kinský Palace** dates from the middle of the 18th century. From the statues on the roof to the Rococo embellishments around the windows, it's an outstanding architectural achievement. The palace is now assigned to the National Gallery's Collection of Graphic Art. Like many of the houses around the square, its basement reveals Romanesque remains.

The **Church of Our Lady of Týn** *(kostel Panny Marie před Týnem)* has visibly stood the test of centuries. Notice how some of the exterior walls are faced with stones of all sizes and shapes. In fact the present Gothic church was built in the middle of the 14th century on the site of a Romanesque structure. This was a church of the reformers even before Jan Hus shook up the religious establishment, but since the Counter-Reformation it has been a Catholic bastion.

The Týn's twin towers, abristle with turrets, are 80 metres (more than 260 feet) tall. They were built in the 15th and 16th centuries. An even older distinguishing characteristic is the northern portal with a tympanum created at the end of the 14th century by Peter Parler's prolific sculptural workshop. Inside, the church is filled with baroque works of art. Facing the main altar, note a **relief** of the Danish astronomer Tycho Brahe (1546–1601), and his tomb. The court astronomer of Rudolph II, Brahe was a stellar figure in medieval science. But he rejected the revolutionary theory of Copernicus, insisting instead that the sun circled the earth.

Another Old Town church of artistic interest, **St. James's** (kostel svatého Jakuba) was founded in 1232, but its ornate appearance dates from the end of the 17th century. St. James's fronts a narrow street northeast of the Týn church, so it's hard to get far enough away from the façade to take in the stucco fantasies of the Italian artist Ottavio Mosto. The interior, fraught with baroque extravagance, is impressive for its sheer size. St. James's Church is also a treat for the ear, with acclaimed acoustics. On Sundays one of the masses features an orchestra and choir.

A historic street, now reserved for pedestrians, runs from the Old Town Square to Republic Square. **Celetná Street** was part of the long route that coronation processions followed from the Powder Tower via the Old Town and Charles Bridge to the castle. The street is lined with grand old mansions, mostly baroque, each worth a close look for the kind of detail that delights the observant eye: the curve of a gable, an unusually shaped window, a wall painting, a statue or an emblem.

An early 20th-century landmark, a six-storey building in cubist style, blends in with the rest of Celetná Street, as if taking its cue from the best of baroque. What's more, the

House of the Black Mother of God (dům U černé Matky boží), an office building named after the religious statue in a corner niche, can hold its own with any contemporary architecture. Note the big bay windows and the mansard roof, as appealing as ever.

The Late Gothic **Powder Tower** (Prašná brána) takes its name from the gunpowder once stored in it. But gunpowder had scarcely been heard of in Europe when the first tower on this site, originally part of the Old Town's defences, was built towards the end of the 13th century. Those were the days of hand-to-hand combats; longer-range service was rendered by spear-throwers and archers. The present tower, surmounting a ceremonial gateway, was begun in 1475 and last renovated in the 19th century. It measures 65 metres (213 feet). At weekends and on holidays, a trickily tight circular staircase inside the tower is opened to the public for a small admission charge; if you're up to it, climb the more than 180 steps to the top for a good 360-degree survey of all the spires of Prague.

Less ancient monument: restored Hotel Paris dates from 1907.

The **Prague Communal Building** *(Obecní dům hlavního města Prahy)*, alongside, is something completely different. Built in the first decade of the 20th century, it's a happy monument to Art Nouveau style. All kinds of amusements from dances to symphony concerts take place here, and the bars and restaurants are steeped in nostalgic atmosphere. On this site stood the royal court of Prague, the residence of several Czech rulers.

Just behind this building and the Powder Tower is Prague's biggest department store, called Kotva (The Anchor). It's worth wandering through this 1970s building to size up the capital's standard of living; Kotva sells everything from food to furniture, and souvenirs, too.

Two buildings cherished as national cultural monuments are situated in the street called **Železná** (the name means "iron"), another of the interesting historic thoroughfares radiating from the Old Town Square. The home of Charles University, the **Carolinum** *(Karolinum* in Czech) was named after Charles IV, who founded it in 1348. Jan Hus served as rector, and after his martyrdom in 1415 the university became a hotbed of the Hussite struggle against the Catholic church.

After the Counter-Reformation triumphed the Carolinum was handed over to the Jesuits. The most pleasing element of the original building still visible is the elegant Gothic **oriel window,** overhanging the street. Imposing, too, is the high-ceilinged Assembly Hall, built in the 17th century. Most of the rest of the complex dates from the 18th century.

With its Neoclassical façade, the **Tyl Theatre** *(Tylovo di-*

Architecture in 3-D

Czech cubist architecture flourished in multi-faceted originality at the very beginning of the 20th century, but only briefly.

The House of the Black Mother of God is the best known example. Another first-rate cubist building is a villa (now an apartment block) facing the river at nábřeží Bedřicha Engelse 26. The three-dimensional sculptural effect of the façade carries over into details inside the house.

A sizeable cubist apartment block by the same architect, Josef Chochol, occupies a difficult corner site in the Vyšehrad district.

Very few cubist projects ever got off the drawing board, for tastes soon changed and Prague turned to modernism.

vadlo) provides a richly historic setting for great occasions. Since its construction in the 1780s, the theatre has had several names. Its present name honours Josef Kajetán Tyl, who galvanized Czech drama in the first half of the 19th century; earlier, German was the usual language of the theatre. In 1787 the Mozart opera *Don Giovanni* received its world première here. Mozart himself conducted the house orchestra. He'd been up most of the night before the dress rehearsal writing the overture.

A one-time Carmelite convent in Rytířská Street, a sizeable baroque presence, now serves as the **House of Soviet Science and Culture** *(Dům sovětské vědy a kultury)*. Tourists may be attracted to the souvenir shop, selling those Russian dolls-within-dolls and Soviet records, and a restaurant where caviar, though cruelly expensive, is as familiar as *bliny* and iced vodka. Just across the street, a late 19th-century neo-Renaissance palace used to be the headquarters of the Prague City Savings Bank and then became the Klement Gottwald Museum, devoted to the first communist president of Czechoslovakia. Now, with the coming of the new Prague Spring, the museum is closed for good.

Josefov

Late in the 19th century Prague's ancient Jewish ghetto, re-named Josefov (Joseph's Town) after Emperor Joseph II, was bulldozed in the path of a bold urban renewal plan. But stately vestiges of centuries of achievement and turmoil remain, making this an essential part of any tour of the city. Synagogues and an amazing cemetery survive, surrounded by a neighbourhood of Art Nouveau apartment blocks erected on the ruins of the medieval warren. The **Museum of Applied Arts** backs on to the old ghetto.

The story of Prague's Jewish community can be traced back to the middle of the 10th century. The city's first known synagogue was built in the 12th century but soon burned down. This fate was typical of the ups and violent downs to follow—fires, restrictive laws and pogroms alternating with periods of relative freedom and creativity. In the darkest age of all, the 20th century, the vast majority of Prague's Jews were annihilated during World War II according to the Nazi master plan. Ironically, priceless monuments were preserved because Hitler wanted relics of his victims catalogued. These were to have been studied as **53** historical curiosities after the proposed extermination of all Jews.

The rather fashionable main street cutting through what used to be the ghetto is **Pařížská třída** (Paris Avenue), where the international airlines and tourist agencies have their offices, and shops with a foreign flair seem to congregate. The avenue runs straight from the Old Town Square to the river; directly opposite, high above the river in Letná Gardens, you can see an unreasonably spacious lookout platform. Until one night in 1962 this mosaic-tiled base supported a statue of Stalin 20 times life size, enjoying an unparalleled panorama of the right bank and St. Vitus Cathedral, on the left bank.

At the opposite end of the avenue, on the edge of the Old Town Square, **St. Nicholas Church** (kostel svatého Mikuláše) once belonged to the Benedictines; now it's a Hussite establishment. Rich baroque details embellish the church, a monument to Kilian Dientzenhofer's talents.

Around the corner, at the crossing of Kaprová and Maislova streets, a modern **bust** of Franz Kafka is attached to the house where he was born in 1883. Kafka is better known in the west than on his home

ground. He wrote in German, in any case, and his nightmarish novels like *The Castle* and *The Trial* weren't translated into Czech until long after his death in 1924. The official perception of his importance in world literature has depended on swings in ideology. The communists banned him in 1948, and again after a thaw in the 60s—his ideas about alienation were deemed subversive.

Kafka is buried in the New Jewish Cemetery. For non-specialist visitors, though, it's the **Old Jewish Cemetery** (Starý židovský hřbitov) to seek out for a haunting experience. (Enter from U starého hřbitova street.) In the shade of tall, wearily leaning old trees sprawls a chaotic jumble of about 12,000 ancient gravestones, all askew. Over the centuries the tombstones were all packed tightly together because, with limited space, the bodies had to be buried several layers deep. The oldest gravestone, belonging to a scholar named Avigdor Karo, is dated 1439; the newest, 1787. The most significant Hebrew inscriptions are explained to visitors taking guided tours. Be sure to have a look at the tomb of the celebrated Rabbi Löw. This 16th-century scholar is remembered as the "father"

of the Golem, a legendary
artificial man, an early prototype of the Frankenstein mon-
ster.

East of the cemetery, the odd-
ly named **Old-New Synagogue**
(Staronová synagóga) was new
when compared with Prague's
original synagogue, but old in
relation to the rest. It is one
of half a dozen historic synagogues comprising the **State
Jewish Museum.** A steeply
pitched roof with Gothic gables
of brick signals this 13th-cen-

*Old Jewish Cemetery: for living
and dead, space is at a premium.*

tury structure, which is taller
than it looks; the floor is
one flight down. High vaulted
ceilings cover its distinctive
twin naves, still the scene of
religious services. Separate
areas for women worshippers
were added in the 17th and
18th centuries. A banner here
(restored in the 18th century)
was presented to the Jews of
Prague by Charles IV in 1358. **55**

Across an alley from the entrance to the Old-New Synagogue, the **High Synagogue** *(Vysoká synagóga)* was one of the achievements of a 16th-century mayor of Jewish Town, Mordecai Maisel. A tireless do-gooder for his constituents, Maisel also served Emperor Rudolph II as minister of finance. The rectangular hall now contains an exhibition covering the history of Jewish arts and crafts. The pink baroque **Jewish Town Hall** *(Židovská radnice)*, abutting the synagogue, is capped by a clock tower. Just below it is another large clock with Hebrew letters denoting the hours; like Hebrew writing, the hands go backwards.

The **Pinkas Synagogue** (under reconstruction), on the far side of the cemetery, began as one family's house of worship in the 16th century. Later, expanded and beautified, it became a fashionable rival to the Old-New Synagogue. After World War II the interior walls were filled with the names of 77,297 victims of the Nazis.

More poignant still is the exhibition in the former **Cere-monial Hall** *(Bývalá obřadní síň)*, next to the cemetery entrance. Tragedy envelops a collection of children's art from the 1940s. Confined to the Theresienstadt concentration camp, the artists pictured their everyday lives behind barbed wire, as well as their dreams. Most of them were to be slain at Auschwitz in 1944.

More Old Town Monuments

The influential theologian Jan Hus, who foreshadowed Protestantism, is remembered in the **Bethlehem Chapel** *(Betlémská kaple)*. This is a reconstitution of the original 14th-century hall in which Hus preached his revolutionary theses. After Hus was excommunicated and executed, the chapel served as headquarters of the Hussite movement. When the Counter-Reformation won control of Bohemia, it was taken over by the Jesuits. Little of the original building was left by the time it was decided to reconstruct it in the 1950s, but some authentic inscriptions have been restored.

The Jesuits were responsible for the **Clementinum** (spelled *Klementinum* in Czech), a complex of buildings so formidable that a whole neighbourhood had to be razed to make room

On the clock of Jewish Town Hall, time marches backwards.

for the project. The monumental baroque façade along Křižovnická Street gives only a hint of its real size. Walk through the courtyards to experience the feeling of immensity of this city within the city, built in the late 17th and early 18th centuries. High above the compound, one of its towers displays the time; the other, called the Observatorium, gave a head start to early 18th-century astronomers. The Clementinum now contains the several

Illuminating: a medieval biblical text in the Clementinum's library.

million books and thousands of rare medieval manuscripts of the State Library of Czechoslovakia.

Facing the eastern tower of Charles Bridge, across a busy road, **St. Saviour Church** *(kostel svatého Salvátora)* once belonged to the Clementinum consortium. But it's older, construction having begun in 1578. It is more inspiring on the inside than its grey exterior might suggest. Built in Renaissance style, it was amended with some effusive baroque afterthoughts.

On Křižovnické Square, **St. Francis Seraphim Church** *(kostel svatého Františka Serafinského)* is the work of a French architect, Jean-Baptiste Mathey. A grand cupola sets the style for this stately structure, built between 1679 and 1689. The inside of the dome is the "canvas" for a huge fresco of the *Last Judgement*.

The majestic **monument** in the middle of the small square features a statue of Emperor Charles IV. It was dedicated in 1848, on the 500th anniversary of Charles University.

From here you'll hardly be able to resist Charles Bridge itself (see p. 38), if only to get a closer look at the Vltava. Another tourist sight in the vicinity is the Smetana Museum.

New Town

Although almost all the medieval monuments have been swept away, Prague's New Town *(Nové Město)* is far older than you may imagine. It was founded by Charles IV in 1348 to ease crowding in the historic core of the city. The district soon became a centre of commerce, where artisans and traders settled and thrived. With its hotels and restaurants, theatres and shops, the New Town is the liveliest part of Prague. Pedestrian zones add to the pleasure of exploring the area.

Wenceslas Square

More a gardened boulevard than a wide open plaza, Wenceslas Square *(Václavské náměstí)* is Prague's answer to the Champs-Elysées, though not so long or wide or fashionable. Find a seat at one of the outdoor cafés facing the square (originally known as the Horse Fair) and watch all Prague stroll past.

Hotels, stores, offices and cinema complexes line the boulevard, which is 60 metres (nearly 200 feet) wide. Almost all the buildings were designed or remodelled in the 20th century; they include some eye-opening examples of Art Nouveau and constructivist style. **59**

At the lower end of the square, the street called **Na příkopě** divides the Old and New towns. Na příkopě, which means On the Moat, was built atop a medieval moat marking the municipal boundaries. Now it's Prague's busiest pedestrians-only street. The tourist agency Čedok operates from a former bank at number 18; the Prague Information Service is at number 20. Among the street's landmarks: several bank buildings in the pompous styles of their eras; a children's department store; a baroque palace now the home of a club and a restaurant; and, always swamped with clients, a fast-food emporium patterned on an American hamburger take-away... but with a diplomatically Russian name.

The street parallel to carless Na příkopě, by contrast clamorous with traffic, is Jindřišská ulice, which cuts across the middle of Wenceslas Square. The main **post office** *(pošta)*, a 19th-century palace, was built on the site of a medieval botanical garden later occupied by a convent. At the far end of the street stands one of the New Town's oldest survivors, **St. Henry's Church** *(kostel svatého Jindřicha)*, begun in the 14th century.

At the top end of Wences-

las Square crowds gravitate towards one of Prague's favourite symbols: the equestrian **statue** of St. Wenceslas himself. This 20th-century monument to the 10th-century prince is by the Czech sculptor Josef Václav Myslbek. Guarding the corners of the pedestal are four other patron saints of Bohemia: Procopius, Adalbert, Ludmilla and Agnes.

You can hardly miss the building looming behind the monument, across the noisy avenue (třída Vítězného února). This immense neo-Renaissance palace, with its great central dome and other heroic touches, has the look of a national capitol building. But it serves as the **National Museum** *(Národní muzeum)*, a role for which it was built at the end of the 19th century. The earth below the museum is now honeycombed with tunnels connecting two Metro lines and offering pedestrian routes to nearby streets and buildings, free of traffic and weather hazards.

Next door, the **Federal Assembly** *(Federální shromáždění ČSSR)* provides a modern contrast. Before World War II, a stock exchange occupied

Wenceslas rides again: monument honours Bohemia's saints.

this site, but the building was too small for the Czechoslovak Socialist Republic's parliamentary needs. In the 1960s, unconventionally if expensively, it was decided to expand the facilities by surmounting the original structure with a second deck on stilts. From the new part, assembly members look out on the cityscape through immense windows.

Two other buildings stand out along the same avenue, the main north-south thorough-

fare. The Neoclassical **Smetana Theatre** *(Smetanovo divadlo),* designed as a venue for German-language operas, has been completely reconstructed in recent times. Now it specializes in Czech operas. The theatre is not to be confused with Smetana Hall, the main concert site in the Prague Communal Building, or, for that matter,

The Polished Polka
Bedřich Smetana (1824–84), father of the Czech school of composition, put the polka into classical music. In *The Bartered Bride,* his most successful opera, he gave new prestige to this vivacious peasant dance. In spite of its name, the polka (meaning Polish girl) is strictly a Czech invention. Legend says it was first improvised by a Bohemian peasant girl around 1830. Within a decade, the rage of Prague was being danced all over Europe, a double-time rival to the waltz.

Another Czech composer who ''borrowed'' the polka, Antonín Dvořák (1841–1904), became internationally renowned for his operas, symphonies, a requiem, and *Slavonic Dances.* Early in his career Dvořák was a violinist in Prague's National Theatre orchestra, conducted, by coincidence, by Maestro Smetana.

the Smetana Museum, alongside Charles Bridge. Prague, clearly, is proud of the great composer, who, like Beethoven, wrote some of his most memorable music after going deaf.

The **Main Rail Station** *(Hlavní nádraží)* is more than just a place to catch a train. A very grand example of Art Nouveau style, it dates from the first decade of the 20th century. Inside, the upper level retains many sumptuous features celebrating the self-confidence of the age of the iron horse.

A ten-minute walk away, among the luxurious old buildings of Hybernská Street, the most pampered is the palace once containing the V.I. Lenin Museum. Built in baroque style in the 17th century, it was re-modelled more than a century

Diva belts out a Dvořak aria for opera fans in Smetana Theatre.

PRAGUE

LITOMĚŘICE

SEDLEC

LYSOLAJE

KOBYLISY

Šárecký p.

TROJA
8 Zoologická
● Zahrada

LIBEŇ

DEVJICE

BUBENEČ

HOLEŠOVICE

LETNÁ

Národní
7 technické
muzeum

KARLÍN

Vltava

VOKOVICE

HRADČANY

Muzeum hlavního
města Prahy
4

JOSEFOV

6 Vojenské muzeum

**MALÁ
STRANA**

STARÉ MĚSTO

ŽIŽKOV

BŘEVNOV

K KARLOVY VARY

NOVÉ MĚSTO

VINOHRADY

1 Faustův dům

Klášter Na Slovanech 2 ●

5 Muzeum Antonína Dvořáka

3 Kostel svatého
Jana Nepomuckého na Skalce

VRŠOVICE

K PLZEŇ

● Bertramka

KOŠÍŘE

Vyšehrad

VYŠEHRAD

NUSLE

ZÁBĚHLIC

RADLICE

PODOLÍ

Botič

JINONICE

MICHLE

Dalejský p.

KRČ

HLUBOČEPY

BRANÍK

**MALÁ
CHUCHLE**

Vltava

HODKOVIČKY

Šeberovský
ryb.

1 Faust House
2 Emmaus Monastery
3 Church of St. John of
  Nepomuk on the Rock
4 Museum of the Capital,
  Prague
5 Antonín Dvořák Museum
6 Military Museum
7 National Technical Museum
8 Zoo

VELKÁ CHUCHLE

MODŘANY

Olšansk

later. In 1912 Lenin himself presided at a meeting of exiled Russians held in the mansion. Now the façade features bas reliefs dramatizing Lenin's life story, ending with a scene of his funeral, Stalin presiding. A similar palace down the street has classical statues on its roof, but the replacements atop the former museum are socialist-realist statues of struggle.

Finally, **U Hybernů House** *(dům U hybernů)*, facing Republic Square *(Náměstí republiky)*, is a haughty example of Empire style. It's the venue for important exhibitions, artistic or technical. U Hybernů (At the Hibernians) was the site of a Franciscan monastery built in the 17th century by monks from Ireland. In their garden grew Prague's first potatoes.

West of Wenceslas Square

Lost in a monastery complex in the middle of the city, the immensely tall, narrow **Church of Our Lady of the Snows** *(chrám Panny Marie Sněžné)* was founded in the 14th century by Charles IV. Despite its impressive dimensions, it never reached the full size of the original Gothic blueprint. A mosaic of *Virgin and Child* on the south façade recalls the art of Byzantine churches; inside there is a splendid baroque

altar. This church was a hotbed of the Hussite movement in the 15th century, when the fiery Hussite priest Jan Želivský preached here. He was the leader of the 1419 raid on the New Town Hall in which rebels jettisoned city councillors, the first of Prague's famous defenestrations.

From here to the river, **National Avenue** *(Národní třída)*, has been a key artery for more than two centuries. Like Na příkopě, this street dividing the Old and New towns follows the course of a moat. A mixed bag of buildings lines the avenue, from baroque palaces to boxy modern glass houses. The biggest of the latter buildings is the Máj (as in May Day) Department Store.

National Avenue's most monumental building, the **National Theatre** *(Národní divadlo)*, is a neo-Renaissance creation of the late 19th century. The architect, Josef Zítek, a professor at Prague Technical University, had to cope with a smallish, irregular site, but he squeezed everything in, to the admiration of most of the citizens. One month before the official opening night in 1881 the roof caught fire, theatrically destroying everything but the walls; throngs came to watch but not the city's firemen, who all happened to be attending a funeral. In the rebuilding, the number of seats was reduced, the number of fire escapes increased. The theatre was again lavishly restored in the 1970s and '80s.

Nová scéna (The New Stage), a modern addition alongside the nation's paramount opera house, has a surprising façade of glass bricks. The theatre, designed for chamber works, seats several hundred people.

If Wenceslas Square is more a boulevard than a plaza, **Charles Square** *(Karlovo náměstí)* is more a park. Prague's biggest square, laid out in 1348, used to be a livestock and vegetable market until it was refurbished with urbanity in the middle of the 19th century. The present grassy park is speckled with fountains and monuments, including a statue of Jan Želivský.

The historic building from which Father Želivský and his co-conspirators defenestrated several municipal officials was the **New Town Hall** *(Novoměstská radnice)*, on the north side of the square. The Hussite raiders also liberated some of their cohorts from the prison on the premises. Very little of the original 14th-century building remains after a series of reconstruction projects over many centuries.

In Resslova Street, west of the square, the baroque **Church of Sts. Cyril and Methodius** *(kostel svatého Cyrila a Metoděje)* is dedicated to the 9th-century monks who brought Christianity to the Slavs. It's the Orthodox cathedral of Prague. But those bullet holes in the wall around the crypt window have nothing to do with religion. In 1942 six Czechoslovak resistance fighters who had parachuted in from Britain died here during a German assault on their hiding place. The team was responsible for assassinating Prague's Nazi overlord, Reinhard Heydrich, nicknamed "the Hangman". Before the siege of the church, the SS had already avenged Heydrich's death by, among other things, obliterating the village of Lidice (see p. 87).

In a choice situation on the east side of Charles Square, **St. Ignatius Church** *(kostel svatého Ignáce)* was built as a Jesuit stronghold. The decoration verges on the Rococo.

Facing Charles Square from the south, **Faust House** *(Fau-*

Islands in the Vltava contribute tranquil touch to central Prague.

stův dům) got its name from the 16th-century legend examined in Goethe's great drama. The connection is as vague as this: the house was occupied by alchemists, and the neighbours suspected that their experiments involved devilishly strange goings-on, even spreading the rumour that Dr. Faust sold his soul to the devil under this very roof. The building itself began as a Renaissance mansion, later going baroque.

A couple of startlingly modern white spires, resembling

Eating on the run in busy Prague; architects pull out all the stops.

rockets frozen in the sky a few seconds after blast-off, mark the former **Emmaus Monastery** *(klášter Na Slovanech)*. The pinnacles provided a daring solution to the problem dropped by American bombers late in World War II when they decapitated the 14th-century church. In its early years this Benedictine monastery aimed to attract Slavs hitherto devoted to the Orthodox faith, so the Catholic mass here was said in Church Slavonic instead of Latin. There are fine, though heavily restored, frescoes in the cloister.

Across Vyšehradská Street from the monastery a lovely ba-

roque church is set on a bluff. Its name is a mouthful: The **Church of St. John of Nepomuk on the Rock** *(kostel svatého Jana Nepomuckého na Skalce).* The architect Kilian Dientzenhofer, who designed this church, was also the author of Prague's most inspired baroque church, St. Nicholas in the Lesser Quarter. Here he

The War Švejk Lost

Jaroslav Hašek was less than 40 years old when he died in 1923, leaving behind an unfinished masterpiece. His book, *The Good Soldier Švejk,* is the riotous saga of a wily warrior, "certified feebleminded", who always succeeds in wearing down the bureaucracy. It has inspired generations of pacifists and downtrodden ordinary people caught in the throes of 20th-century life. And few books have so effectively undermined the myths surrounding the heroics of warfare.

Hašek wrote from personal experience. He served in the Austrian army during World War I and was taken prisoner by the Russians. Another similarity to his fictional hero: Hašek sometimes earned money peddling dogs with bogus pedigrees. Then came the disillusionment of the dogs of war.

surmounted the problem of a steep, narrow site with a high-flying church of theatrical symmetry.

Dientzenhofer also gets credit for **Villa Amerika,** a delightful mansion in a little park of its own in Ke Karlovu Street. The American connection is indirect: apparently there used to be an inn nearby named "America". The building now serves as the **Antonín Dvořák Museum.** By coincidence, Dvořák spent several years in the United States, where he was inspired to compose his best-known symphony, *From the New World.*

Around the corner in Na bojišti Street, a tavern called **U kalicha** (The Chalice) is usually chock-a-block with tourists who have come to eat pork ribs and dumplings, drink beer and pay tribute to a sort of war hero. In this beer hall the quintessential Czech hero, the fictional Good Soldier Švejk, spent many happy hours before "intervening" in World War I. In the book he tells an army acquaintance on the way to the front, "When the war's over come and see me. You can find me every evening from six o'clock at The Chalice..." In real life, Švejk's creator, Jaroslav Hašek, was an inveterate client here.

Vyšehrad

As in the days of the mystical Princess Libuše, who foresaw Prague's greatness many centuries ago, there's a choice view over the Vltava from the cliff's edge at Vyšehrad. In spite of its legendary connection with the princess, the right-bank fortress is probably only the second oldest part of the city. King Vratislav II moved here from the earliest Prague castle, Hradčany, in the 11th century. Less than a century later the court was transferred back across the river. Even so, Vyšehrad (High Castle) retained at least ceremonial importance: the long coronation processions through the whole city and up the hill to Prague Castle used to start here. The present fortress walls were begun in the reign of King Charles IV. Otherwise, not much of irresistible interest remains, except for an ancient chapel, a neo-Gothic church and a celebrated cemetery.

The oldest building of Vyšehrad, **St. Martin's Rotunda** *(rotunda svatého Martina)*, is a Romanesque round chapel of the 11th century. Like many a venerable building it suffered the indignities of history. Somewhere along the line military priorities transcended religious needs, and the chapel was turned into a gunpowder magazine. But its architectural importance was rediscovered late in the 19th century, and the rotunda was restored.

The **Church of Sts. Peter and Paul** *(kostel svatého Petra a Pavla)* looks as old as the Middle Ages, but its landmark towers are 20th-century versions of Gothic architecture. Closer to the ground, authentic Gothic elements remain. Mosaics on the façade give it an eastern touch. Outstanding among the works of art inside, a Gothic painting of the Virgin dates from the 14th century.

The idea of visiting a cemetery may leave you cold, but **Vyšehrad Cemetery** *(Vyšehradský hřbitov)*, next to the church, is no ordinary graveyard. Some of the tombs here are the necropolitan equivalent of the mansions the rich burghers enjoyed in life. Look over the sculptural effusions, the floral offerings, and the names, which comprise a roll of honour of leading Czechoslovakian citizens, including Dvořák and Smetana.

Over the Bridge

A lot of water has flowed under the bridge since Charles IV built his sturdy span across the Vltava. And a number of newer bridges now stand shoulder to shoulder along the river, but **71**

Prague's most original modern bridge crosses no river. The **Most Klementa Gottwalda** strides efficiently across the populous Nusle Valley. A six-lane highway occupies the top level of the bridge, which is 500 metres (more than 1,640 feet) long, while in its streamlined underbelly runs a Metro line. Passengers deprived of the scenery get their reward at the Vyšehrad metro station, which is above ground and all view.

The station leads to the **Prague Palace of Culture** *(Palác kultury Praha)*, the capital's prime venue for events ranging from political rallies to concerts. The main Congress Hall seats more than 2,800 delegates or music-lovers, as the case may be, and there are smaller halls for other functions. The first event held under the palace's roof, when it opened in 1981, was the 16th Congress of the Communist Party of Czechoslovakia.

Across the busy highway, a modern skyscraper hotel offers additional conference facilities. The **Hotel Forum Praha** has more than 500 guest rooms and services like a communications centre and car wash, saunas, squash and bowling. And tourists are tempted with Prague's first gambling casino.

Museums

Prague's museums concentrate on themes as broad as literature or as narrow as the life and work of a single composer. As for art, galleries little heard of abroad show to good advantage an unsuspected wealth of old masters, even older masters, and modern works as well.

Here's a rundown of the principal museums of Prague.

In a neo-Renaissance palace backing on the old Prague ghetto, the **Museum of Applied Arts** *(Uměleckoprůmyslové muzeum)* at 17. listopadu 2, Prague 1, highlights the craftsmanship of old and modern masters of Czech crystal, porcelain and woodcarving. Confirming the importance of beer in local society, there are enormous illustrated beer mugs from the 16th and 17th centuries. See, too, the domestic and foreign achievements in clockmaking, cabinetmaking and bookbinding.

Bertramka is the name of the villa where Mozart lived on various occasions late in the 18th century, most notably when readying the première of *Don Giovanni*. In a wooded estate near the peaceful Malá Strana cemetery, the little museum displays historic scores and letters and musical instruments. The street address, appropriately, is Mozartova 169, Prague 5. Opening hours are as eccentric as a left-handed fiddler: check before you go.

The **Museum of the Capital, Prague** *(Muzeum hlavního města Prahy),* in sady Jana Švermy, Prague 8, presents the city's turbulent history in uncluttered, graphic style. The displays include prehistoric tools and inspired Gothic sculpture. Upstairs the centre of attraction is a remarkably complex, homemade model of the city of Prague as it looked in the early 19th century.

The **Muzeum Antonína Dvořáka** in Villa Amerika, a small red palace at Ke Karlovu 20, Prague 2, honours Czechoslovakia's best known composer. Dvořák (1841–1904) was widely honoured in his lifetime, as is well documented here. You can see the cap and gown he wore when he received an honorary doctorate from Cambridge University in 1891. On show, too, are his original scores, quill pen, walking sticks and eyeglasses, and souvenirs of the time he lived in the unlikely town of Spillville, Iowa.

Before its closure, the **Klement Gottwald Museum** (Rytířská 29, Prague 1) had an impressive approach to its main exhibition—a 50 step, red-carpeted climb up to a statue of Lenin. Relics of Gottwald, Czechoslovakia's first communist prime minister and president, included three unsmoked pipes and a fur hat. The museum also covered the selective history of the Communist Party of Czechoslovakia.

The **Jewish Museum** *(Státní židovské muzeum)* has its own version of a diaspora. The exhibits (closed Saturdays and Jewish religious holidays) are distributed among several buildings in the Josefov quarter, including historic synagogues. The Klaus Synagogue contains documentation on the arts and religious practices of Prague's ancient Jewish community. The best of the exhibits were gathered during World War II, when the Nazis zealously searched out every last ethnological detail about a people they planned to eliminate.

The **Muzeum V. I. Lenina** (Hybernská 7, Prague 1—now closed) had room after room of exhibits on the life and work of the communist leader who became the Soviet Union's first head of state. A prime attraction was the conference room where Lenin met with some of his exiled compatriots in 1912.

Historic Strahov Monastery, south-west of Hradčany, is the 73 striking setting for the **National Literature Museum** *(Památník národního písemnictví)*. Booklovers, whether or not they understand Czech, will love the museum's display of precious old books and manuscripts—illuminated psalters, hymnals, and scientific treatises. Museum-lovers will be fascinated by the anteroom to the glorious Philosophical Hall, where cases of seashells, rare pottery and butterflies constitute an 18th-century prototype of a museum.

The striking Renaissance Schwarzenberg Palace, just outside the walls of Prague Castle, now serves as command post and parade ground of the **Military Museum** *(Vojenské muzeum)*. Considered one of the most comprehensive of its kind in the world, the collection starts with an axe head from around 3000 B.C. and works its way through the evolution of weaponry to 20th-century cannon. Along the way are guns and banners from what's called here the "French Bourgeois Revolution" of 1789.

The **Museum of Musical Instruments** *(Muzeum hudebních nástrojů)*, facing Knights of Malta Square in the Lesser Quarter, assembles an appealing array of clavichords, harpsichords and pianos from the 18th and 19th centuries, when, it seems, the beauty of the box was as important as the music it produced.

The building of the **National Museum** *(Národní muzeum)*, at the top end of Wenceslas Square, sums up the adjective "palatial". It's a good place to remember on a Monday, the day when almost all the other museums in Prague are closed. The historical department runs from prehistoric discoveries to interesting World War II relics. Under the same roof, the Museum of Natural Sciences is an old-fashioned collection of animal, vegetable and mineral specimens.

The main building of the **National Gallery** *(Národní galerie)* is the former Sternberg Palace, almost hidden behind the Archbishop's Palace. The address is Hradčanské náměstí 15, just outside the walls of Prague Castle. Don't be discouraged by the roundabout entranceway that looks as if you're using the servants' door; just follow the signs. The Collection of Old European Art, meaning 14th through 18th centuries, excludes Bohemian artists, who rate their own

Words and pictures: illustrated ceiling spans Strahov's library.

museum. Outstanding here are the Italian Renaissance paintings, Byzantine and Russian icons, and rare German and Flemish works. Among the best-known painters represented are three dynasties: the Brueghels, the Cranachs and the Holbeins. A position of honour is given to Dürer's *Madonna of the Rose Garlands,* considered the first (1506) group portrait in German art. For a new viewpoint on Prague note the cityscapes painted in 1934 and '35 by the Austrian Oscar Kokoschka—colours you never noticed, making the Vltava River come alive. Across the courtyard, on the ground floor, a prize collection of 19th- and 20th-century French art features most of the Impressionist greats plus Picasso and Braque.

The National Gallery's **Collection of Old Bohemian Art** *(Sbírka starého českého umění)* fills three floors of the thousand-year-old former Convent of St. George, inside Prague Castle. Among hundreds of works, largely on religious themes, the most extraordinary are a set of icons by Master Theodoric. These works, from

It all started here: Cranach view of Eden in the National Gallery.

Karlštejn Castle, blaze with innovations—bright colours, soft outlines, realistic forms; the pictures even "bleed" into the frames. Among Czech baroque painters, it's well worth discovering the portraits of Karel Škréta, Jan Kupecký, Petr Brandl and Anthony Kern.

In a far corner of the Old Town, the Convent of the Blessed Agnes *(Anežský klášter)* is now the distinguished Gothic home of the National Gallery's **Collection of 19th-century Czech Painting.** The pictures on show sum up the trends of the century in all its variety—from Romanticism to Symbolism. The ground floor is assigned to the Czech decorative arts and crafts of the 19th century—splendid crystal and porcelain.

Another former convent, the Karlov Monastery in the New Town, houses the **Museum of the National Security Corps** *(Muzeum SNB a vojsk MV).* This unusual institution documents the exploits of the troops assigned to keep Czechoslovakia's frontiers impermeable.

The **Prague Castle Picture Gallery** *(Obrazárna Pražského hradu)* in the Second Courtyard of the castle, displays a few dozen outstanding paintings by old masters. The collection was begun in the 16th century by a

Tourist ponders Picasso nude in National Gallery collection.

reclusive art-lover, Rudolph II, the emperor who moved his capital from Vienna to Prague. Most of Rudolph's paintings were carried off as war booty in 1648; you'll have to go to Stockholm to see them. Of special interest here are works by Rubens, Tintoretto, Titian and Veronese.

The **Muzeum Bedřicha Smetany** (Novotného lávka 1, Prague 1), dedicated to the life and works of Bedřich Smetana, isn't likely to thrill any but **78** serious fans of the composer.

Most of the displays consist of family photos, original scores, and newspaper reviews in Czech. But the situation, on a mini-peninsula alongside Charles Bridge, and the neo-Renaissance building are perfect (closed Tuesdays).

Prague's **National Technical Museum** *(Národní technické muzeum)*, in a 1930s building a bit out of the way at Kostelní 42, Prague 7, contains hundreds of thousands of utilitarian objects, many thoroughly fascinating. The historic exhibits are a reminder that Czechoslovakia was a foremost power in European technology before World War II.

Excursions

Organized day-trips from Prague emphasize the grandeur of Czech castles, which come in all models from stark Gothic forts to baroque pleasure palaces. Other highlights are historic towns and famous spas. Along the way to these cultural rendezvous, relish the restful scenery of Bohemia's fields and forests.

Here's a rundown, in alphabetical order, of the principal excursion stops within striking distance of Prague:

Český Šternberk

The solid, Gothic Český Šternberk castle has glared down over the Sázava River, southeast of Prague, since the reign of the first King Wenceslas in the 13th century. Within the impregnable-looking walls, though, a lot has changed. The baroque interior decorations are rich in generous details: flamboyant chandeliers, elegant furniture and, above all, outstanding stucco work.

The *štern* in Šternberk comes from the German *stern* (star). This is alluded to in star motifs which turn up everywhere in the castle—in the design of parquet floors, for instance, and in the tiles of the beautiful old stoves. The castle has a hoard of hunting trophies, including an open-jawed stuffed crocodile on the floor. You, too, will gape when you sight the view of the forested hills from the castle's library—a panorama to distract the most dedicated bibliophile.

Hluboká Castle

Renovation in the 19th century turned this ancient fortress into a crenellated construction like a child's toy castle. You half expect to see it guarded by miniature soldiers in bearskin hats. The decorations tend towards the overwhelming; keeping track of the ceilings alone is a major undertaking.

Just north of České Budějovice, the capital of South Bohemia, Hluboká Castle dominates the strategic Vltava River. Its dramatic history begins in the middle of the 13th century. One of the castle's early owners, named Záviš of Falknštejn, lost a political struggle, and the property, and his life: in 1290 he was executed in a meadow in the shadow of the castle. After some interim zigzags the castle came into the Holy Roman hands of King Charles IV.

In the 16th century the original Gothic castle was transformed into a Renaissance château. When the baroque craze came in, the place was rebuilt. **79**

The owners were the Schwarzenberg family, German nobles who prospered in the service of the Habsburg dynasty. They soon acquired more property than any other landlords in Bohemia, and kept it until nationalization after World War II.

The final facelift for Hluboká Castle, begun under Johann Adolf II of Schwarzenberg in the mid-19th century, was inspired by the Gothic style. To enhance the romantic effect, an unusually spacious English garden was created.

On the way into the complex, a hunting motif is as subtle as a blast from a blunderbuss: sculpted deers' heads project from the walls in the courtyard, but the antlers are real. Among the castle collections are medieval weapons and knights' armour. On another plane there are precious tapestries and antique furniture. To house all this, no expense was spared, from the parquet floors to stuccoed ceilings.

The former stables now contain a worthy collection of Bohemian art, mostly medieval religious works. Flemish and Dutch paintings of the 17th century round out the display. You enter through a "winter garden" reminiscent of a Victorian glasshouse.

Karlovy Vary

Thanks to its handsome site and salubrious mineral springs, Karlovy Vary in western Czechoslovakia has attracted an illustrious crowd of health faddists down through the centuries. Dropping a few historical names: Bach, Goethe, Gogol, Liszt, Brahms and Grieg came here, along with political figures from Czar Peter the Great to Karl Marx.

Gone, alas, is the glamour of pre-war days. Most of the curists sucking hot water from their special spouted cups look glumly ill or convalescent, and socially a long way from the old crowd of crowned heads, nabobs and snobs. Still, the stately spa town, hidden in a ring of richly wooded hills, is a pleasant outing in nostalgia.

Karlovy Vary (formerly known as Karlsbad) is named after Charles IV, who put his imperial seal of approval on the spa in the 14th century. Members of his hunting party, rushing after a deer, are said to have discovered the first hot spring, and soon medieval medicine men were prescribing the waters for many ailments. The early patients had to spend hours every day bathing in the hot springs, as well as bloating themselves drinking the health-giving water. Nowadays the **81** treatment is more selective and less draconian.

Going from fountain to fountain (walking is as important as drinking) people taking the cure can admire the town's architectural landmarks. The **Church of Mary Magdalene** *(kostel Maří Magdalény)* was designed in the 1730s by Kilian Dientzenhofer of Prague baroque fame. The filigreed wooden **Market Colonnade** has been eclipsed by the Neoclassical **Colonnade** (formerly called the Czechoslovak Soviet Friendship colonnade). And the newest attraction for the mineral-water version of a pub-crawl is the modern **Yuri Gagarin Colonnade,** with a geyser wheezing, spitting and exploding in its own rotunda. Here the taps flow with water from various local sources, at natural temperatures as hot as 72 degrees Celsius (162 degrees Fahrenheit). Generally it tastes either rusty or boring—not everybody's cup of tea.

As in the great old days of Karlsbad the balneological equivalent of après-ski activities are supposed to be as stimulating as the treatments. Karlovy Vary has an international film festival, concerts and theatrical programmes, an art gallery, and many cafés and restaurants. Shoppers can dab-ble in porcelain and glassware, the local liqueur (called the "13th curative spring") and the highly prized wafers of Karlovy Vary, which taste like virgin ice-cream cones.

Karlštejn Castle

The Holy Roman Emperor Charles IV, who transformed Prague into a capital of European culture, built this classic castle to protect the crown jewels behind walls six metres (20 feet) thick. For added security he chose a sheer hilltop site in pine-forest country 28 kilometres (17 miles) south-west of Prague. Hrad Karlštejn, the most visited monument beyond the city limits, is everybody's idea of a medieval castle.

In spite of its impregnable air Karlštejn developed a certain vulnerability. It survived with less than flying colours a protracted siege by powerfully armed Hussite rebels in 1422. Again, in a footnote to the Thirty Years' War, Swedish attackers gravely damaged the castle in 1648; Charles IV couldn't have anticipated the power of modern field artillery,

This Karlovy Vary café recalls the mood of Karlsbad's heyday, when royalty "took the waters".

which the Swedes pioneered. A serious restoration project finally got underway late in the 19th century.

The **Imperial Palace** *(Císař-ský palác)* only one of several imposing buildings behind the crenellated walls, now displays historical exhibitions largely devoted to the life and times of the founding emperor. In the king's audience hall, the original wood panelling of the walls and ceilings has been restored. In an early example of royal one-upmanship, the throne was positioned to let glaring sunlight intimidate visitors who dared to look the monarch in the eye. Luxembourg Hall contains a tapestry version of the family tree of the

Emperor Charles IV built Karlštejn Castle to safeguard the crown jewels. But, despite appearances, the fortress proved vulnerable.

house of Luxembourg, including Charles and his four wives. And on the walls hang many royal portraits.

Some precious Gothic wall paintings have been discovered in the **Church of Our Lady,** including scenes featuring Charles himself. Connected to this small church is a much smaller **Chapel of St. Catherine,** the emperor's private retreat, its walls studded with semi-precious stones.

In the castle keep, the

Holy Cross Chapel *(Kaple svatého Kříže)* was the repository of the crown jewels and other irreplaceable regalia. Behind the altar, too, were preserved the most vital state documents. The state treasures were symbolically protected by a "heavenly army" of more than 100 saints as portrayed in thoroughly remarkable paintings by the 14th-century court artist, Master Theodoric. His technique seems to have leaped centuries ahead of his time. (The originals are now displayed in the National Gallery's Collection of Old Bohemian Art in Prague.)

Konopiště Castle

Like Karlštejn, Konopiště began as a bristling Gothic fortress. But this lion ended up as a lamb, or a lap-dog: a hunting lodge for the ill-fated heir to the Habsburg throne.

Forty-four kilometres (27 miles) south of Prague, Konopiště was built in the late 13th century in the style of a French fortress. The layout of towers, walls and moats made it all but unbeatable as a redoubt. By the 17th century, though, the Swedish army showed how warfare had changed, and Konopiště fell.

Early in the 18th century the Count of Vrtba bought the

place and began revolutionary renovations. In the vulnerable castle's new pacific mode, Konopiště became the baroque country home of a noble family. Then in 1887 the Austrian Archduke Franz Ferdinand took over the property, which he greatly expanded and improved.

Franz Ferdinand was noted for his love of hunting. He was, in fact, a fanatic. He gunned down almost anything with four feet or two wings, even the most inoffensive little beasts and birds. Thousands of his trophies cover the walls of this ostentatious lodge.

Franz Ferdinand also collected armour. The display at Konopiště is as varied and impressive as you'll find in any castle in Europe. It includes gorgeous horse-and-rider armour for ceremonial jousts, and anything a knight might need from pikes to mini-cannon.

The archduke, as is well known, met his destiny at the other end of a gun. His assassination at Sarajevo in 1914 precipitated World War I. Austria-Hungary lost. During World War II, when the castle was requisitioned by occupying SS troops, many Konopiště treasures found their way to Germany, but all have been

recovered.

Kutná Hora

Like Tombstone, Arizona, and Taxco, Mexico, the Czech town of Kutná Hora was built on silver. Founded in the 13th century, when apparently bottomless silver deposits were discovered nearby, Kutná Hora soon experienced the joys and growing pains of a boom town. Situated about 65 kilometres (40 miles) south-east of Prague, it became the country's second most important town in the Middle Ages.

On a bluff overlooking the town, **St. Barbara Cathedral** *(chrám sv. Barbory)* looks as if it is about to soar heavenwards, buttresses, spires and all. Its High Gothic lines were designed late in the 14th century; construction went on until the middle of the 16th century. The extravagance of the architecture and furnishings testifies to the glitter of the town's silver heyday. Kutná Hora's silver connection is evident, too, in a set of frescoes in the cathedral showing miners and minters at work.

The façade of the oldest house in town, called the **Stone House** *(Kamenný dům)*, is adorned with exuberant stonework and an inspired oriel window. Another fine relic is the decorative 15th-century town well. Nobody is allowed

recovered.

to tamper with the appearance of the historic centre of Kutná Hora, all Gothic and baroque buildings.

The **Italian Court** (the Czech name is *Vlašský dvůr*) was a project of King Wenceslas II. Here, from the very beginning of the 14th century, the local silver was processed into Prague *groschen,* coins that were recognized as legal tender all over Central Europe. The Italian element in the name refers to the expert minters who were recruited to start production; Italian bankers followed. So did French technicians, specialists in silver casting and minting. Incidentally, the bottom dropped out of the silver business here in 1726, when the mint closed down for lack of raw materials. The most opulent part of the building is the Assembly Hall, with a splendid medieval ceiling.

Lidice

The pilgrimage to Lidice, only 22 kilometres (14 miles) northwest of Prague, is no joy ride. It's a poignant little history lesson, as profound as the grave.

Lidice was an undistinguished Czech mining village until 1942,

Eyewitness to an atrocity: one of the survivors, in Lidice museum.

when Hitler ordered it "liquidated" to discourage further resistance. Wiping Lidice off the map—figuratively and cartographically—was a well-publicized reprisal for the assassination of SS-Obergruppenführer Reinhard Heydrich. Gestapo and SS troops rounded up the inhabitants, about 450 in all, and burned down every house. They shot all the men (and a few women), sent the remaining women and some of the children to concentration camps, and handed over other, racially acceptable children for adoption by German families.

A lovely green hillside marks the place where the village stood, with a clump of cedars shading the mass grave. Overlooking the site is a small museum containing photos of the victims and mementoes such as bullet-riddled identity cards. Look at the faces of the women who work in the museum, selling tickets or mopping the floor. They survived the slaughter.

Mariánské Lázně

Like Karlovy Vary, Mariánské Lázně is a spa with a romantic history. Cultural celebrities like Goethe, Turgenev, Ibsen, and Kafka used to gravitate to Marienbad, as it was then known, to soak up the beneficial waters as well as inspiration. Goethe, for one, fell in love on the spot, with a girl who was much too young, prompting him to write *Marienbader Elegie*.

In the far west of the country, just across the border from West Germany, Mariánské Lázně is founded on water—bubbling mineral springs—but the ozone-rich air is also said to be unusually healthful. There are well over a hundred local springs, of which 40 are credited with therapeutic value. Patients are supposed to spend three weeks in this beautifully landscaped array of 19th-century baths and sanatoria. The cure involves drinking oceans of water, bathing in it, and digesting it while walking at length through the gardens and the forests beyond. There are also mud-baths and injections of carbonic gas bottled at the springs.

As a counterpoint to the serious business of health, wholesome distractions are encouraged. The intellectual tone of the old days is maintained, to an extent, with events such as an international music festival and frequent theatrical presentations. Less highbrow are the golf competitions and fashion shows.

Mělník

This hill town stands atop the vineyards descending in their disciplined ranks to the junction of the Elbe *(Labe)* and Vltava rivers, 32 kilometres (20 miles) north of Prague. (Pointing to the relative size of the rivers at this peaceful spot, the locals claim the Elbe is a tributary of the Vltava and not the other way around, as geography books state.)

Legend says the 9th-century Princess Ludmilla originated the idea of using these lands for wine. Charles IV added expertise, importing vines from Burgundy. In spite of this long history, the wines of Mělník are virtually unheard of abroad. That's no reason to turn down a tasting in a cool cellar or a cheerful tavern, or both.

The grandest local landmark, impressive on its hilltop, is **Mělník Castle** *(hrad)*. It now serves as a museum and art gallery.

A tall Romanesque tower stands alongside the Gothic Church of Sts. Peter and Paul *(kostel svatého Petra a Pavla)*. Inside, a bizarre **ossuary** is crammed with tens of thousands of skulls and bones. The scene is not only grisly, it's fascinating, for the skeletal relics have been painstakingly arranged in artistic patterns.

Slapy Dam

By car, bus and boat, holidaymakers from Prague head south to relax at Slapy Dam, on the Vltava River. It's also a customary stop on excursions to nearby Konopište Castle.

Building the dam, which took four years, changed completely the look of the countryside. The dam created an artificial lake 40 kilometres (25 miles) long. While waiting its chance to turn the turbine to produce electric power, the Vltava water also serves many recreational purposes, such as boating, fishing and swimming. And just surrounding beautiful embracing islands that used to be mere hills.

Tábor

On the edge of the town of Tábor, 88 kilometres (55 miles) south of Prague, an artificial lake called Jordan is said to date back to the historically eloquent year of 1492. The Hussites used Lake Jordan for baptismal purposes, hence the biblical name. (Tábor itself is named after Mount Tabor in Galilee, biblical scene of a great Israelite victory over the Canaanites.)

The Hussites, members of a religious and political reform movement, split into two factions early in the 15th century. **89**

The more militant ones were called Taborites, referring to the town they made their headquarters. Tábor was well fortified in anticipation of attack by anti-reformist crusaders of the Holy Roman Empire; the streets of the old town are still laid out in a maze to make the way more difficult for invaders.

The **town square**, Žižkovo náměstí, honours Jan Žižka, the Hussite military chief, who was based here. This splendid, spacious square looks eminently peaceful, but tunnels and cellars were dug beneath it for use in a siege. The Gothic **town hall** is largely dedicated to a museum of the Hussite movement, with considerable documentation about Žižka, the one-eyed military genius. (But statues, paintings and the portrait of him on the 20 Kčs banknote can't agree as to which eye was covered with a patch.) Architecturally, the most remarkable aspect of the town hall is its vast ceremonial chamber, unmarred by supporting columns. It may be the mightiest non-royal, non-ecclesiastical hall of its era.

Damming the Vltava created Slapy Lake, a recreational wonderland.

What to Do

Entertainment

Whether your mood veers towards frivolous or cultural diversions, Prague is well equipped to entertain you. From discos to grand opera, from cabaret to drama, you'll be exhausted long before you exhaust the capital's possibilities. For a complete rundown on the more serious attractions, look for the leaflet of coming events, issued monthly in English, French and German editions by the Prague Information Service. It's free at hotels or information offices.

Music has been one of Prague's strong points ever since Mozart and Beethoven used to captivate the local audiences. (So did Liszt, Berlioz, Wagner and Tchaikovsky.) Almost any evening there's a choice of glamorous musical events: the Czech Philharmonic Orchestra, one or two of the local chamber music ensembles, as well as opera programmes competing with one another at the National Theatre and the Smetana Theatre. Generous government support for the arts means tickets are cheap. The musical pace picks up every year be-

tween May 12 and June 4 during the Prague Spring International Music Festival, a hectic pageant of local and foreign orchestras and ensembles, with celebrity soloists and conductors. The venues include historic churches and palaces.

The **theatre** scene is always busy. The featured playwrights include Sophocles and Shakespeare, Tennessee Williams and Edward Albee. The catch is that the language is normally Czech, so you may be deflected

Ingenious special effects, widely copied elsewhere, were originated by Prague's Magic Lantern team.

to one of the pantomime theatres or—quite possibly the best show in town—*Laterna Magika*. If any of the techniques of the multi-media Magic Lantern spectacle seem familiar, consider that they were invented here, beginning in the 1950s. The exciting mixture of music, mime, ballet and film, surrealism, humour and philosophy is always a sellout. But if you don't mind a substantial mark-up, consult the ticket scalpers who congregate outside.

Folklore performances are presented daily at 7.30 p.m. during July and August on Slovanský Island (near the National Theatre). Each of Czechoslovakia's regions—Bohemia, Moravia and Slovakia —has its own music, dances and costumes.

Nightclubs cater to distinct moods and age groups. In the cabarets, variety acts and song-and-dance routines (long-legged showgirls and all) are interspersed with dancing to live music. Noisier are the discos and video discos. It all goes on until 2 or 3 in the morning. For more sedate nightlife you can find piano bars and candle-lit wine restaurants *(vinárny)* with soft music and good food.

Cinemas abound around Wenceslas Square. Foreign films are often shown in the original version with Czech subtitles. Avoid the movies listed with a small square symbol alongside the title; regardless of the original language they have been dubbed into Czech. Seats are reserved, so it's best to book early.

For Children

The Prague **Zoo** *(Zoologická zahrada)* will engross children of all ages. The spacious, forested setting, out of the way in Troja, Prague 7, gives a certain freedom to the more than 2,000 animals. The most unusual inhabitants are the Przewalski horses, handsome, white-muzzled natives of Asia, now extinct in the wild but bred here.

Boat trips on the Vltava start from the quay just north of Palacký Bridge. The excitement attracts dozens of friendly swans, who graciously accept handouts. The excursion itineraries, subject to river conditions, are suspended in winter. Farther north, on Slovanský Island (near the National Theatre) rowing boats may be hired.

A favourite place for Prague children is the 19th-century **maze** *(bludiště)* in Petřín Park, near the local imitation of the Eiffel Tower. There is a mirrored labyrinth and a gallery of curved mirrors, always echoing with delighted laughter. The exciting way to get there is by funicular up the hillside (see p. 44).

Older children will enjoy several of Prague's **museums,** such as the National Technical Museum with its historic bicycles, cars, trains and planes. **93**

Sports

For a small country Czechoslovakia produces an improbably plenteous crop of international **tennis** stars. Their names, however complex, trip from the tongues of sports fans everywhere. The secret, apparently, is a rigorous nationwide talent hunt and training programme, a modern approach to a traditional Bohemian sport (the first tennis tournament hereabouts was held in 1879).

To see the future stars practicing, have a look at the big modern tennis complex on Štvanice Island, in the Vltava River beneath the Hlávkův Bridge, south-east of the Praha-Expo 58 restaurant. You may be able to play there, too, but only by reserving a court in advance (tel. 23 16 323).

As for **golf,** there's a nine-

Czechoslovakia didn't invent tennis, but many aces started here.

hole course at Motol (Prague 5). More elegant is the 18-hole layout at the historic spa of Mariánské Lázně (Marienbad).

The country's leading **spectator sports** are ice hockey, football (soccer), basketball and volleyball. The last word in sports stadiums is the Strahov installation in Břevnov, Prague 6, possibly the world's biggest. For gymnastic occasions there's room enough on the field for 16,000 sportsmen. The adjoining football stadium seats a mere 56,000 spectators.

Horse racing takes place every Sunday from April to the end of October at Chuchle, with small-scale betting at the track. Every October a famous steeplechase is run, about 80 kilometres (50 miles) east of Prague, at Pardubice. More than 50,000 spectators come out to watch the race, perchance to wager a few crowns on the outcome.

Hunting, a favourite pastime among Czech royalty of old, is organized by Čedok. Package tours are available in which everything is included: accommodation, transport, guide and gun. From birds of a feather to bears (in the mountains of Slovakia), the range of targets is wide. Except for early spring, some type of game is in season most of the year.

Shopping

In some cities—Rome, London and Hong Kong, for example—shopping is one of the main events. Prague is not in the same league, but that doesn't mean you won't enjoy a good look around the department stores and boutiques. The window-shopping is particularly pleasurable along the "King's Road" of Prague, the progression of historic streets leading from the Powder Tower in the Old Town all the way to Prague Castle.

For an over-all picture of what's for sale in Prague, take your own unguided tour of one of the big department stores, Kotva or Máj. Along with toothpaste and light bulbs they sell furniture, clothing, sports equipment, and even souvenirs for tourists.

Handicrafts ranging from bric-à-brac and trinkets to fine embroidery and ceramics are sold at state-run shops with names like ÚVA, Zádruha, Krásná jizba, Česká jizba, and Dílo (the last specializing in works of art).

In various parts of town you'll find Tuzex stores, each devoted to specific kinds of merchandise from cameras to clothing. Prices in Tuzex stores are marked either in Czechoslovakian koruna (Kčs) or, more likely, in Tuzex hard-currency units, abbreviated Tk. Prices quoted in the latter monetary unit must be paid for in foreign currency or by credit card. The exchange rate is less favourable than the tourist rate. Anything purchased in a Tuzex store can leave the country duty-free. Save all receipts.

For most gift buyers, Czechoslovakia means **crystal** and **glassware.** The best-known brand names are Moser (founded in Karlsbad in the mid-19th century) and Bohemia.

Porcelain is another promising area. If you're not in the market for a 110-piece, hand-painted dinner service, consider a porcelain figure. There's a choice of subjects: birds, or a brace of hunting dogs, or nudes, pensive or ecstatic.

Among shopping ideas: marionettes and tasty bottled souvenirs.

Hand-made **marionettes** are widely available, representing dramatic or melodramatic figures, including favourite opera characters. And there are plenty of **dolls** in regional costumes. And carved wood dolls and angels.

Embroidery is well represented in the gift shops, especially tablecloths and napkins in folkloric patterns.

And look for Bohemian **garnets** *(České granáty)*—clusters of semi-precious stones made up into brooches, bracelets or chains.

For a liquid souvenir, consider a **bottle** of *Becherovka*, the aperitif from Karlovy Vary ("since 1807"), or one of the more powerful Czechoslovakian drinks, such as *slivovice* (plum brandy).

Finally, Prague being such a musical capital, the **discs** and **tapes** make interesting souvenirs. Lend an ear to the locally produced classics, opera, folklore and pop.

Eating Out

Prague offers the perfect antidote to the rigours of health food and *nouvelle cuisine:* honest, filling, often delicious dishes, based on the kind of recipes grandmother kept to herself. You'll never go away hungry.

The hearty Czech cuisine typically centres on roasted pork or beef with, almost inevitably, dumplings to soak up the gravy. Or your appetite may point to poultry, game or freshwater fish. The generally heavy, savoury food goes down best of all with cold Czech beer, a brew admired for centuries by experts everywhere.

The atmosphere in Prague's eating places is often colourful or romantic. The service, though, can be unpredictable. The waiters may be friendly or efficient, and sometimes both, but in some restaurants the employees, who prefer to relax at mealtimes, all but ignore the customers.

Where to Eat

Eating places, of which Prague has a couple of thousand, are divided into categories and then graded from one plus (luxurious) to four according to the level of the facilities. For technical reasons many a good restaurant gets no more than a second-class seal of approval (written *II. cenová skupina*); don't let that put you off.

Apart from conventional restaurants *(restaurace),* which may be posh or geared to a regional or foreign cuisine, look for these options:

Vinárny ("wine restaurants") may have the same menus as ordinary restaurants but they emphasize the wine accompanying the food. The atmosphere is often intimate, perhaps historic or folkloric.

Pivnice (pubs or taverns) specialize in draught beer and a limited variety of food; the mood is likely to be jolly, with informal service.

Kavárny (cafés) are essentially for snacks and pastries rather than for hot meals.

If you're in a rush you can eat very cheaply in a *jídelna,* a rather spartan self-service eatery (cafeteria), sometimes furnished only with stand-up tables, to speed the turnover.

Anti-smoking activists will be pleased with Prague, where smoking in restaurants tends to be banned at lunchtime. This doesn't affect pubs, however.

Winning combination at a Lesser Quarter café: historic buildings, fresh air and a thirst-quencher.

Breakfast

Hotels serve breakfast *(snídaně)* from about 6 to 10 a.m. Depending on the establishment the meal can be as simple as bread, butter and jam with coffee or tea, or as bountiful as you could wish. In the better hotels they serve a lavish hot and cold buffet big enough to affect your lunch plans.

Lunch and Dinner

Most restaurants post a typewritten menu *(jídelní lístek)* near the door, giving you an idea of the prices, at least. At the self-service counter you needn't know the language; just point to what you want. At the other end of the scale, first-class restaurants normally have menus in several languages. Between the extremes of luxury and economy, ordinary restaurants issue the menu in Czech only. Try it. But don't make a scene if the waiter, on the assumption that no foreigner can read a Czech menu, declines to show it to you. He would prefer to discuss the food with you... in German. Many Czechs seem to suppose that all foreigners know German. If you don't, perhaps English can help.

The menu is divided into categories like these: *studená jídla* (cold dishes), *polévky* (soups), *teplé předkrmy* (warm starters, or appetizers), *ryby* (fish), *drůbež* (poultry), *hotová jídla* (main courses) and *moučníky* (desserts).

The supreme **starter** here is Prague ham *(pražská šunka)*, a succulent local speciality. It may be served in thin slices, garnished with cucumber and a horseradish sauce, or with cheese in miniature sandwiches.

The Dumpling Situation

If you thought dumplings were golf-ball-sized portions of dough with no more flavour than a paste-pot, you're in for a revelation in Prague. You may even become a dumpling expert, discussing the pros and cons of flour dumplings as opposed to potato dumplings, and which gravy is best to surround them.

The ubiquitous dumplings of Prague come in several varieties: the small spheres made of flour or potato batter; big dumplings speckled with bread bits, served in slices; big dumplings, also sliced, containing chunks of bacon; and the dessert version, stuffed with plums, with sweetened curd cheese (cottage cheese) on top.

The bitter pill is that, as you search for the very best dumpling in town, you may become as round as a dumpling yourself.

Soup is popular at both lunch *(oběd)* and dinner *(večeře)*. It may be a fairly light bouillon or, more likely, a thick, wholesome soup combining potatoes, vegetables and perhaps a bit of meat. Don't be shocked if a dab of whipped cream is added. One of the great traditional recipes is *bramborová polévka s houbami* (potato soup with mushrooms). The name hardly does justice to the thick soup flavoured with onion, lard, carrots, cabbage, parsley and spices.

Meat dishes include *Pražská hovězí pečeně* (Prague roast beef), a joint of beef stuffed with fried diced ham, peas, egg, onion and spices. And look for *svíčková pečeně na smetaně*, tasty beef in a cream sauce. Some hotel restaurants offer an inspired variant on a simple theme, *vepřové žebírko Interhotel* (pork chops à l'Interhotel), the chops stuffed with a mixture of sauerkraut, ham and bacon. Another gourmet adventure is *šunka po starочesku* (old Bohemian-style boiled ham), involving a sauce of plums, prunes, walnut kernels and wine. Or for memories of the Austro-Hungarian Empire, try *guláš* (goulash), a meat stew with paprika sauce, or *smažený řízek* ("Wienerschnitzel"), a breaded veal cutlet. Just about any of these dishes may be accompanied by *knedlíky* (dumplings) and *kyselé zelí* (sauerkraut).

Desserts gravitate towards the heavyweight category, with satisfying ideas like *jablkový závin* (apple strudel), probably served with a topping of whipped cream. A slightly more delicate variation, *jablka v županu* (apple baked in flaky pastry), uses entire peeled apples stuffed with sugar, cinnamon and raisins. *Švestkové knedlíky* (plum dumplings) are sprinkled with sieved curd cheese and sugar, then doused in melted butter. Or settle for *zmrzlina* (ice-cream) or *kompot* (stewed fruit).

Snacks

Between meals in Prague you'll be tempted by an inventive array of inexpensive snacks sold at street stands. A *bramborák* is a potato pancake, served greasily but deliciously on a piece of paper. *Pečená klobása* (roast sausage) rates a paper plate, a slice of bread and a squirt of mustard, but no fork or knife. *Smažený sýr* is a sort of vegetarian Wienerschnitzel. And ice-cream is sold everywhere, most commonly from hole-in-the-wall cone dispensaries offering only one flavour per day. Shop around!

Beer and Wine

When the international statisticians turn to **beer** *(pivo)*, Czechoslovakia usually comes in among the top two or three countries in the world for per capita consumption. Once you taste the local brew on the spot you'll know why.

The kind of connoisseurs who go to Burgundy for wine-tasting pilgrimages should go to Plzeň (Pilsen), in western Czechoslovakia, for the beery equivalent. Pilsner beer, produced since the 13th century, is a species of lager admired and copied far and wide. Experts attribute its special flavour to the alkaline water and the ex-

cellence of a key ingredient, hops, which grows on vast wood-and-wire frames all through the Bohemian countryside. (The plants climb the wires like Jack's beanstalk.)

Pilsner beer is the best known, but there are well-regarded breweries in Prague and smaller towns. Several Prague pubs brew their own, light or dark. As tasty and refreshing as the chilled nectar may be, keep in mind that it's probably stronger than what you're used to.

Czechoslovak **wine** *(víno)* is almost unknown abroad, so you're bound to discover something new. If you like it, thank Charles IV for importing vines from Burgundy in the 14th century. Nowadays Bohemia produces only a small proportion of the country's total wine output, most coming from Slovakia and Moravia. Bohemian wines (from the area of Mělník, notably) are reminiscent of German wines. White is *bílé* and red is *červené.*

A herbaceous drink from Karlovy Vary, *Becherovka,* is served chilled as an aperitif, as is the powerful, sweetish *Stará myslivecká.* After-dinner drinks usually mean fruit brandies, especially *slivovice*, made from plums.

Non-alcoholic drinks include therapeutic mineral water, fruit juices, and internationally known, rival colas. In the coffee department, Italian-style espresso competes with thick Turkish coffee.

Well-balanced waiter rushes cold clear beer to his thirsty clients. 103

To Help You Order...

Could we have a table?
The bill, please.
I'd like...

Máte prosím volný stůl?
Zaplatím.
Prosím...

beer	**pivo**	meat	**maso**
bread	**chleba**	the menu	**jídelní lístek**
butter	**máslo**	milk	**mléko**
cheese	**sýr**	mineral water	**minerálku**
coffee	**kávu**	salad	**salát**
dessert	**moučník**	sugar	**cukr**
egg	**vejce**	tea	**čaj**
ice-cream	**zmrzlinu**	wine	**víno**

...and Read the Menu

bažant	pheasant	**knedlíky**	dumplings
brambory	potatoes	**králík**	rabbit
drůbež	poultry	**kuře**	chicken
fazole	beans	**květák**	cauliflower
houby	mushrooms	**kyselé zelí**	sauerkraut
hovězí	beef	**ledvinky**	kidneys
hrášek	peas	**pstruh**	trout
hrozny	grapes	**rajská jablka**	tomatoes
hrušky	pears	**rýže**	rice
husa	goose	**špenát**	spinach
jablka	apples	**srnčí**	venison
jahody	strawberries	**štika**	pike
játra	liver	**šunka**	ham
jazyk	tongue	**švestky**	plums
jehněčí	lamb	**telecí**	veal
kachna	duck	**telecí brzlík**	sweetbreads
kapr	carp	**vepřové**	pork
klobása	sausage	**zajíc**	hare

BLUEPRINT for a Perfect Trip

How to Get There

As fares and routes are constantly changing, it's best to consult a dependable, well-informed travel agent for up-to-date information. The following outline suggests some of the varied possibilities.

BY AIR

Scheduled flights. Prague-Ruzyně airport is well served on international and intercontinental routes by the Czechoslovakian airline ČSA and foreign companies.

Flying times: New York–Prague 10½ hours; London–Prague 2 hours.

Package tours. The all-in package tour—flight, hotel and board included—proves a popular way of visiting Prague. Take your choice of a wide variety of packages, from short breaks to a grand tour of Czechoslovakia, with Prague as a point of departure. Most tour agents recommend cancellation insurance, a modestly priced safeguard: you lose no money if illness or accident forces you to cancel your holiday.

North American packages featuring a visit to Prague include air fare, transfers, accommodation, sightseeing, and some or all meals. Many tours are organized around a theme (Czechoslovakian composers) or event (the Prague Spring festival, for example).

BY CAR

The most convenient route to Prague is the E-12 (Frankfurt–Nuremberg–Pilsen), crossing the border at Waidhaus-Rozvadov (open round the clock). You can also follow the E-15 via Berlin, Dresden and Karl-Marx-Stadt, entering Czechoslovakia at Schmilka-Hřensko (open 24 hours).

BY RAIL

Service is good on the Ostend–Prague line, linking Paris, Strasbourg, Stuttgart and Nuremberg. Departures are frequent from Frankfurt, Munich and Vienna, less so from Rotterdam. Travellers from London will have to change trains in one of the cities mentioned above.

Note that western European rail passes like the Inter-Rail card, Rail Europ S card and Eurail pass are now valid for travel in Czechoslovakia.

By car ferry from the British Isles and Ireland. It's 1,200 kilometres (745 miles) from London to Prague, a long haul across the Channel (opt for the Dover–Ostend ferry) and on through Belgium and Germany.

When to Go

Prague is a four-seasoned city with a continental climate. The summers tend to be sunny and quite hot, the winters cold, spring and autumn mild but changeable. The hotels are usually packed from April to mid-November and also during festivals and congresses, so advance planning is essential.

Some Prague averages*, month by month:

		J	F	M	A	M	J	J	A	S	O	N	D
Maximum	°F	49	53	64	73	82	88	91	89	84	71	57	50
	°C	10	11	18	23	28	31	33	32	29	22	14	10
Minimum	°F	7	10	18	29	36	44	49	47	38	29	24	14
	°C	−13	−12	−8	−2	2	7	9	8	4	−2	−5	−10

*Minimum temperatures are measured just before sunrise, maximum temperatures in the afternoon.

Planning Your Budget

To give you an idea of what to expect, here's a list of average prices in Czechoslovakian koruna (Kčs) and U.S. dollars, However, remember that all prices must be regarded as *approximate*.

Airport transfer. ČSA bus from Prague-Ruzyně airport to Vltava Terminal 6 Kčs. ČSA-Čedok bus from airport to selected hotels 100 Kčs. Taxi from airport to central Prague 140 Kčs.

Buses and metro. Standard fare 1 Kčs per trip. 24-hour pass valid on all lines and vehicles 8 Kčs, 48-hour pass 15 Kčs, 72-hour pass 20 Kčs.

Car hire. *Skoda* US$33 per day, $198 per week, plus $0.33 per km. *Renault* medium size $45 per day, $270 per week, plus $0.45 per km. *Renault* automatic or *Opel Omega* $55 per day, $330 per week, plus $0.55 per km. Insurance liability waiver $10 per day.

Cigarettes (packet of 20). Local brands 8–14 Kčs, foreign brands not available in local stores.

Entertainment. Opera 30–60 Kčs, concert 50–100 Kčs, nightclub admission 40–50 Kčs, disco admission 40 Kčs.

Hairdressers. *Woman's* shampoo and set 60 Kčs, blow-dry 70 Kčs, cut 35 Kčs, permanent 200 Kčs. *Man's* haircut 35 Kčs.

Hotels (double room with bath, including breakfast). A* de luxe US$238, A* US$172, B* US$148 (half-board), B US$35 (half-board, without bath).

Meals and drinks. Lunch/dinner in fairly good restaurant 300 Kčs. Coffee 12 Kčs. Glass of wine 20 Kčs. Soft drink 10 Kčs. Beer 12 Kčs.

Taxis. Meter drops at 6 Kčs. Panorama Hotel–Wenceslas Square 25 Kčs. Railway station–Ethnographic Museum (Smíchov) 30 Kčs.

Tours. City sightseeing (three hours) 200 Kčs. Prague by Night (dinner included) 550 Kčs. All-day tours to Bohemian castles 500–600 Kčs.

An A–Z Summary
of Practical Information and Facts

Listed after some entries is the appropriate Czech translation, usually in the singular, plus a number of phrases that may come in handy during your stay in Czechoslovakia. For a guide to pronunciation, see under LANGUAGE.

ACCOMMODATION. Hotels are officially classified according to the scope and standard of their services, from "A* de luxe" at the top, through A*, B* and B to a very modest "C". (Sometimes the scale is symbolized by stars—five for the most luxurious, one star for the most basic.) To earn the A* de luxe rating a hotel must have superior rooms and elaborate facilities of the sort international businessmen expect, such as translation and secretarial services, a fitness centre, shops on the premises, and multiple bars and restaurants. If you're aiming down a notch or two to A* or B*, you won't be roughing it. And some hotels with fewer stars outdo the posh modern palaces in architectural charm and friendly service. But "C" class hotels truly have no frills.

Package tours usually include breakfast and dinner or full board; in some cases the commitment may be reduced to breakfast only

It's advisable to book accommodation well in advance, as the principal hotels are often filled to capacity. Only a few periods of the year are relatively slack—for instance darkest winter, when group rates are lowered as an incentive. If you arrive without a reservation, go to the main reservation centre of Čedok, the country's biggest travel agency, at Panská 5, Prague 1, or to Pragotur, U Obecního domu 2, Prague 1.

Botels. For an efficient alternative to a conventional hotel you can stay in a converted river-boat, called a "botel". Prague has three of these floating hotels permanently moored along the Vltava. The amenities rate three stars.

Campsites, aimed at economy-minded vacationers, are found in several areas near central Prague, such as Trója and Braník. Don't

A

expect luxury: the standard of services is rated no higher than average. To make reservations drop by the Pragotur office, U Obecního domu 2, Prague 1 (opposite the Hotel Paříž).

I'd like a single room/ double room.	**Chtěl bych jednolůžkový pokoj/dvoulůžkový pokoj.**
with bath/with shower	**s koupelnou/se sprchou**
What's the rate per day?	**Kolik stojí za den?**

AIRPORT *(letiště)*. Prague-Ruzyně airport, less than 20 kilometres (12 miles) from the city centre, is served by the Czechoslovakian airline ČSA and more than 20 foreign lines. In addition to its international role, Prague is the transit point for flights to Bratislava, Brno and lesser airports around the country.

Facilities include a bank, accommodation bureau, post office, car hire desk, café and restaurant. There are souvenir and duty-free shops. Luggage trolleys (baggage carts) are free, and there are porters on hand to help with your luggage.

Ground transport. Taxis by the dozen are available for arriving passengers. Apart from public buses, ČSA runs a special bus service between the airport and the Vltava Terminal, at Revoluční 25, by the river. It departs at least half-hourly until 7 p.m. Another airport bus, run by ČSA and Čedok, serves several principal hotels four times per day.

Departure. For the correct check-in time, consult your airline or the ČSA office. If you arrive at the airport early or your flight is delayed, you can pass the time in the transit area in a cinema (no admission charge). Travel films about Czechoslovakia are shown with English narration.

Where do I get the bus to the city centre?/to the airport?	**Odkud jede autobus do centra města?/na letiště?**
Porter!	**Nosič!**
Take these bags to the bus/taxi, please.	**Prosím, odneste tato zavazadla k autobusu/taxi.**

C

CAR HIRE *(půjčovna auto)*. See also DRIVING IN CZECHOSLOVAKIA. In Prague the choice of car rental agencies narrows down to Pragocar, the local representative of Avis, Budget, Europcar, Hertz and Inter-

Rent. The International Reservation Office is at Štěpánská 42, Prague 1, telephone 23 52 809 or 23 52 825. Other Pragocar offices are located at the airport and the Hotel Inter-Continental.

Pragocar rents a wide range of economy and luxury cars, both Czechoslovakian and foreign. You have the choice of a standard tariff per hour or day and an unlimited-mileage rate including collision damage waiver. The requirements and paper-work are about the same as in any other country, with the most convenient method of payment by credit card. But Czechoslovakia has this particularity: it's illegal to drive with even a drop of alcohol under your belt.

I'd like to hire a car.	**Chtěl bych si půjčit auto.**
large/small	**velké/malé**
for one day/a week	**na jeden den/týden**
Please include full insurance.	**Prosím, započítejte plné pojištění.**

CIGARETTES, CIGARS, TOBACCO *(cigareta, doutník, tabák).* Tobacconist shops (look for the sign "Tabák") usually offer a full range of cigarettes, local and imported, as well as cigars (including expensive Cuban brands) and pipe tobaccos.

Restrictions on smoking in public places are becoming more widespread. Smoking is prohibited on all local public transport and in Prague railway stations. There is, however, a smoking section on trains. In most restaurants smoking is banned between 11 a.m. and 2 p.m.

I'd like a packet of cigarettes.	**Prosím krabičku cigaret.**
filter tipped/without filter	**s filtrem/bez filtru**
light tobacco/dark tobacco	**světlý tabák/tmavý tabák**
A box of matches, please.	**Prosím krabičku zápalek.**

CLOTHING. In summer lightweight clothing is recommended, though a jacket or sweater might come in handy in the evening. Winters are cold, so you'll need an overcoat and heavy shoes. Rainwear is useful much of the year.

Casual attire is fine for most occasions, though business circles tend towards sober suits. In the evening a certain amount of formality is appropriate, especially if you're going to the opera or the theatre, where local women sometimes wear evening clothes. Incidentally, public places have vast cloakroom (hatcheck) facilities, which should be used. It's considered *nekulturní*—literally "uncultured"—to wear or carry a hat or coat into a restaurant or theatre. Some establishments insist on coats being handed in.

COMMUNICATIONS

Post offices *(pošta)* handle mail, telegrams, telex and telephone service. Postage stamps are also available where postcards are sold. Post boxes, attached to buildings, are either orange facing the street but blue on the sides, with a slot in each of the sides or (the more modern ones) all yellow with two slots in the front, at the top. Mail to Europe takes three to five days, to North America seven to ten days. The historic main post office at Jindřišská 14 (Prague 1) is open 24 hours a day. They still offer clients the use of pens and ink bottles—just as they did in the days before the ballpoint started rolling.

Poste Restante/General Delivery. If you're going to be in Prague long enough to receive mail, but don't know where you'll be staying, you can have letters addressed to you Poste Restante (the same expression is used in Czechoslovakia as in Britain). Pick up your mail at the main post office. Don't forget to take along your passport for identification.

Telegrams *(telegram)* may be sent from any post office and from most hotels.

Telex service is available at the main post office and at principal hotels.

Telephone *(telefon)*. Coin-operated telephones are found on the street, in Metro stations (your best bet for a phone in working condition) and other public places. Two principal types of public telephone are in operation. The simpler model can be used for local calls only. A very complicated, outsize variant serves for both local and international calls (have plenty of coins at hand). In both cases, elaborate illustrated instructions are posted. The basic coin valid in all the machines is the 1 Kčs piece, but if the cash-box is full your contribution will be rejected at the crucial moment, cutting the line. For international calls without the coin problem try any post office or your hotel.

express (special delivery)	**expres**
registered	**doporučeně**
air mail	**letecky**
I'd like a stamp for this letter/ postcard, please.	**Prosím známku na tento dopis/ lístek.**
I'd like to send a telegram.	**Chci poslat telegram.**
Can you get me this number in ...?	**Můžete mne spojit s tímto telefonním číslem v ...?**

COMPLAINTS. If you feel you have been badly served or over-charged, ask for redress on the spot; talk politely but frankly with the manager or director of the hotel, restaurant or shop. If this fails to bring satisfaction, ask to write your grievance in the complaint book *(kniha přání a stížností)*. Every enterprise must keep such a book available for its clients. Simply threatening this serious escalation, suggesting many bureaucratic complications, usually brings results.

CONSULATES and EMBASSIES *(konzulát; vyslanectví, velvysla-nectví)*. To find the address and telephone number of any diplomatic representative in Prague look in the telephone directory under "Zastu-pitelské úřady". The main ones for English-speaking visitors:

Canada	Mickiewiczova 6, Prague 6; tel. 32 69 41
United Kingdom	Thunovská 14, Prague 1; tel. 53 33 47
U.S.A.	Tržiště 15, Prague 1; tel. 53 66 41

CONVERSION CHARTS. For fluid and distance measures, see p. 117. Czechoslovakia uses the metric system.

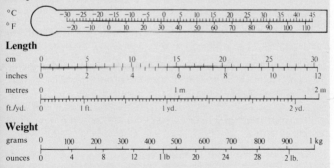

Temperature

Length

Weight

COURTESIES. Hand-kissing is a vanished custom, but other tradi-tional Central European niceties still pervade Prague life. Handshakes all around open and close any meeting, business or social. For busi-ness meetings, punctuality is appreciated. If invited to homes, a gift of flowers or a bottle of good wine would be appropriate.

C **CRIME and THEFT.** Violent crime is still rare by the standards of western Europe or the United States, but thefts do happen. Lock your car and put your valuables in the hotel safe. Be alert to the danger of pickpockets in crowded places.

Don't become a criminal yourself: changing money on the black market is an offence in Czechoslovakia.

I want to report a theft.	**Chci ohlásit krádež.**
My wallet/handbag/passport/ ticket has been stolen.	**Ukradli mi náprsní tašku (peněženku)/kabelku/pas/ lístek.**

CUSTOMS *(clo)* **and ENTRY REGULATIONS.** Advance planning is necessary for a trip to Prague. You need a passport (it must be valid for at least another five months) and a Czechoslovakian visa. Visas are not issued at the frontier or the airport on arrival, with the exception of the Rozvadov crossing point on the Nurnberg-Plzeň-Prague route, where visas can be issued. Otherwise, apply to a Czechoslovakian embassy or consulate before you go. You have to provide your passport, a completed application form (available from some travel agencies), two passport photos, and a visa fee. A visa is normally valid for one visit of up to 30 days.

You are permitted to bring into Czechoslovakia personal effects for use during your visit, though valuable cameras and the like should be declared on arrival. Gifts, too, can be imported without paying duty, so long as they are of reasonable quantity and value. Beyond the familiar prohibitions, such as drugs and firearms, pornographic books or publications may not be imported.

Currency restrictions. There is no restriction on the amount of foreign currency you're allowed to take into or out of Czechoslovakia. However, no Czechoslovakian currency may be imported or exported.

On arrival at the airport the first stop is the bank, where you must change some money into Czechoslovakian koruna or you won't be permitted through the police entry control. Generally, foreign visitors are required to change the equivalent of 30 West German marks (15 marks per child aged 6-15 years) per day at the basic exchange rate. For anything over this amount, the rate is doubled—in your favour. The exception is tourists arriving with vouchers proving that hotel services have been paid for in advance. These vouchers can **114** be obtained through travel agents.

Registration. When you check into your hotel, you have to hand over your passport, which may not be returned until the next day. (Don't forget to ask for it.) During this time it will be registered with the police. Visitors staying in a private household must register themselves, within 48 hours of arrival, at the Public Security Office, Olšanská 2, Prague 3. Here are some of the items you can take into Czechoslovakia duty-free and, when returning home, into your own country:

Entering Czecho slovakia	Cigarettes	Cigars	Tobacco	Spirits	Wine
	250 or similar quantity			1 l. and	2 l.
Into:					
Australia	200 or	250 g. or	250 g.	1 l. or	1 l.
Canada	200 and	50 and	900 g.	1.1 l. or	1 l.
Eire	200 or	50 or	250 g.	1.l. and	2.l.
N. Zealand	200 or	50 and	250 g.	1.1 l. and	4.5 l.
U.K.	200 or	50 or	250 g.	1 l. and	2 l.
U.S.A.	200 and	100 and	*	1 l. or	1 l.

*A reasonable quantity.

On departure, there's a tight limit (500 Kčs) on the amount of purchases you can take out of Czechoslovakia, with the exception of items purchased with hard currency at Tuzex shops or by credit card. So keep your receipts. It is forbidden to export antiques, many foodstuffs, furs, shoes and children's clothing, unless they were acquired through Tuzex.

I have nothing to declare.	**Nemám nic k proclení.**
It's for my personal use.	**To mám pro osobní potřebu.**

DRIVING IN CZECHOSLOVAKIA

Entering Czechoslovakia. To bring your own car into the country you will need:

D

- a valid national licence and an international driving permit
- car registration papers
- a form obtainable along with the visa
- Green Card (an extension to your regular car insurance policy, validating it specifically for Czechoslovakia)
- a national identity sticker for the car
- a first-aid kit
- a red warning triangle for use in case of breakdown

If you're driving someone else's car, you must have the owner's written permission.

At the border you must buy **petrol coupons** *(poukázka na benzin)*. Petrol cannot be sold at pumps for cash. Check the latest situation when you arrange your trip.

Speed limits. The maximum is 110 kilometres per hour (68 mph) on main highways, 90 kph (56 mph) on other roads, and 60 kph (37 mph) in towns. The limits are rather strictly enforced. The police levy fines on the spot; ask for a receipt.

Driving conditions. Drive on the right, pass on the left. Seat belts must be worn at all times. Alcohol is totally forbidden to drivers; if any amount, however small, is found in the bloodstream it constitutes a serious offence.

For the uninitiated driver, Prague is an obstacle course. Pedestrian zones, one-way streets, detours and construction projects mean that only people with endless time to spare and expert knowledge—for instance, taxi drivers—feel comfortable driving here. It's even worse during the rush hours, from 6 to 8 a.m. and from 3 to 5 p.m. In view of the congestion, deviations and parking restrictions, visitors are advised to leave their cars outside the centre of Prague and take public transport from there.

Breakdowns. The "yellow angels", mobile mechanics of Autoturist Road Service, come to the aid of motorists in distress. There are some 20 garages for repairs around the country, two of them in Prague. Look for emergency telephones on the highway, or dial 158 for the police.

Fuel and oil *(palivo; olej)*. Most service stations are open from 6 a.m. to 8 or 9 p.m., but 24-hour stations operate in several districts of Prague. Fuel comes in four varieties—special (90 octane), super (96 octane), diesel and (less widely available) unleaded.

Fluid measures

imp. gals. 0 .... 5 10

litres 0 5 10 20 30 40 50

U.S. gals. 0 .... 5 10

Distance

km 0 1 2 3 4 5 6 8 10 12 14 16

miles 0 ½ 1 1½ 2 3 4 5 6 7 8 9 10

Parking. Prague is trying to provide adequate space for all the cars in short- and long-term car-parks in or near the central district. There are also some "human parking meters" who collect a fee for on-street parking. But if you leave your car in a restricted zone it may be towed away.

Road signs. Most road signs are standard international pictographs, but here are some written ones you may come across:

Jednosměrný provoz	One way
Na silnici se pracuje	Road works (Men working)
Nebezpečí	Danger
Nevstupujte	No entry
Objížďka	Diversion (Detour)
Opatrně	Caution
Pěší zóna	Pedestrian zone
Pozor	Attention
Snížit rychlost (zpomalit)	Slow down
Vchod	Entrance
Východ	Exit

Full tank, please.	**Plnou nádrž, prosím.**
super/normal/unleaded/diesel	**super/obyčejný/bezolovnatý/ nafta**
Check the oil/tires/ battery, please.	**Prosím, zkontrolujte mi olej/ pneumatiky/baterii.**
I've had a breakdown.	**Mám poruchu.**
There's been an accident.	**Stala se nehoda.**
Can I park here?	**Mohu zde parkovat?**
Are we on the right road for...?	**Jedeme dobře do...? (Vede tato silnice do...?)**

117

E **ELECTRICITY.** In almost all the places a tourist might alight in Prague the power is 220-volt, 50-cycle A.C. American appliances will need transformers and plug adaptors.

EMERGENCIES. In an emergency you can phone the following numbers 24 hours a day:

Police	158
Fire	150
Emergency first aid	155
Ambulance	373333

Careful!	**Opatrně!**
Fire!	**Hoří!**
Help!	**Pomoc!**
Stop thief!	**Chyťte zloděje!**

G **GUIDES and TOURS.** Čedok operates a wide range of multilingual guided tours of short and long duration, from a three-hour orientation tour of Prague to excursions all around Czechoslovakia. The agency can also arrange an individual guide/interpreter. Some of the hotels, as well as Čedok, can provide qualified translators or interpreters for business visitors.

H **HAIRDRESSERS and BARBERS** *(kadeřník; holič)*. The traditional separation between men's and women's hairdressing establishments persists in Prague. However, some gentlemen's barbers are women. A 10% tip is usually appropriate.

shampoo and set	**umýt a natočit**
blow-dry	**foukaná**
permanent wave	**trvalá**
colour rinse	**přeliv**
manicure	**manikůra**
Not too short.	**Ne moc krátké.**
A little more off (here).	**Trochu víc ubrat (tady).**

HEALTH and MEDICAL CARE. Emergency medical care is provided free of charge to foreign visitors. Beyond the emergency stage, a charge is made for medical treatment, except for citizens of countries with reciprocal agreements on medical treatment. There is a clinic for foreigners at Palackého 5, Prague 1. For emergency medical aid, telephone 155. For an ambulance, dial 333. Emergency dental treatment is available at Vladislavova 22, Prague 1.

Certain pharmacies *(lékárna)* are open after normal business hours; to find the shops on night duty, look for the addresses posted on the door of any pharmacy. If you require certain medicines it's wise to bring an adequate supply from home, for equivalents may not be available in Czechoslovakia.

Where's the nearest pharmacy?	**Kde je nejbližší lékárna?**
I need a doctor/dentist.	**Potřebuji lékaře/zubaře.**
I have a pain here.	**Bolí mne tady.**
headache/stomach ache	**bolest hlavy/žaludku**
fever/cold	**teplota (horečka)/rýma**

HOURS. The working day begins early in Prague. Food shops start opening up from 6 a.m. and may not close until 6 p.m. Department stores and certain other shops do business from 8 a.m. to 7 p.m. Small shops close for a long lunch hour, but the big stores work non-stop. Most stores are open Saturday mornings, but Sunday is an almost universal day of rest.

Banks operate from 8 a.m. to noon and 1 to 5 p.m., Monday to Friday.

Museums tend to be open from 9 or 10 a.m. to 5 or 6 p.m. daily except Mondays.

LANGUAGE. The national languages are Czech and Slovak, which are related and mutually intelligible. The most widely studied foreign languages are English, German and Russian. If Slavic languages are Greek to you, a notion of German will take you farthest. Most people in Prague seem to know more than a smattering of German, and assume that all foreigners do, too. English is the next best bet, particularly among younger people and in establishments catering to tourists.

The Czech alphabet has 33 letters; for instance, *c* and *č* are counted as two different letters. Here are a few tips on the pronunciation of the more difficult sounds:

ť like *ty* in not yet	**č** like *ch* in church
ň like the *n* in Canute	**ch** like English *h*
š like the *sh* in shine	**j** like *y* in yellow
ž like the *s* in pleasure	**ř** like *rs* in Persian
c like *ts* in tsetse	

119

L

Do you speak English?	**Mluvíte anglicky?**
I don't speak Czech.	**Nemluvím česky.**
Good morning/Good afternoon	**Dobré jitro/Dobré odpoledne**
Good evening/Good night	**Dobrý večer/Dobrou noc**
Please	**Prosím**
Thank you	**Děkuji Vám**
Thank you very much	**Velice Vám děkuji**

LAUNDRY and DRY-CLEANING. The easiest way to deal with the problem is to hand over your laundry to your hotel maid. Less expensively, you can patronize the neighbourhood laundry *(prádelna)* or dry-cleaner *(čistírna)*. Express laundries can wash, dry and press your clothes within 24 hours. Even more expeditiously, several of Prague's dry-cleaning establishments provide while-you-wait service. But coin-operated launderettes are rare.

When will it be ready?	**Kdy to bude hotovo?**
I must have this for tomorrow morning.	**Musím to mít na zítra ráno.**

LOST PROPERTY. The Lost Property Office *(Ztráty a nálezy)* is at Bolzanova 5, Prague 1, tel. 23 68 887. A separate office specializing in lost documents is at Olšanská 2, Prague 3, tel. 24 51 84.

I've lost my passport/wallet/handbag.	**Ztratil jsem pas/náprsní tašku (peněženku)/kabelku.**

M

MAPS *(mapa, plán).* The travel agency Čedok issues free maps of Prague. More detailed city maps are sold at newsstands. And bookshops sell an official town plan in book form, dissecting Prague into 81 pages of detailed maps with an index of all street names and voluminous lists of useful addresses.

The maps in this book were prepared by Falk-Verlag, Hamburg.

a street plan	**plán města**

MONEY MATTERS

Currency. The unit of currency in Czechoslovakia is the *koruna* (crown), abbreviated *Kčs.* The koruna is divided into 100 *hellers (hal.).*

Coins: 5, 10, 20, 50 hal., 1, 2, 5 Kčs.

Notes: 10, 20, 50, 100, 500, 1,000 Kčs.

120   For currency restrictions, see CUSTOMS AND ENTRY REGULATIONS.

Currency-exchange offices *(směárna)* at the frontier, the airport, and in town at banks, travel agencies and hotels, give tourists a bonus on the official rate of exchange. When changing money you'll have to show your passport with visa and currency-exchange documents.

Black market money-changers infest tourist areas of Prague; from all sides the German word *Tauschen* (exchange) is whispered in your ear as secretly and enticingly as "massage" in Bangkok. Beware: "unofficial" money changing is not allowed in Czechoslovakia.

A variation on Czechoslovakian currency: Tuzex vouchers, valid for purchases in the ubiquitous Tuzex hard-currency shops, are issued in various denominations of Tuzex koruna (abbreviated *TK*). These can be obtained abroad or from various banks and exchange offices in Prague. The problem is that they cannot be changed back into the original currency. Therefore, it's better to use Western money, or Charge Cards, in the Tuzex shops.

Traveller's cheques may be changed at banks and currency-exchange offices. They are also accepted in Tuzex shops and certain tourist restaurants. You'll be asked to show your passport when cashing a cheque.

Credit cards. The main international credit cards are accepted at Tuzex shops, Čedok offices and principal hotels and restaurants. Be sure to save all receipts, which you may be required to show on departure.

I'd like to change some pounds/dollars.	**Chci vyměnit nějaké libry/dolary.**
Do you accept traveller's cheques?	**Berete (Přijímáte) cestovní šeky?**
Can I pay with this credit card?	**Mohu platit touto úvěrovou kartou?**

NEWSPAPERS and MAGAZINES *(noviny; časopis)*. If you can read German, you'll be able to catch up with local cultural, touristic and television highlights in the weekly *Neue Prager Presse*, distributed free at hotels and Čedok offices. Otherwise, foreign-language news is available in limited quantities in hotels and in a state-owned store specializing in foreign newspapers and magazines at Jungmannova 5, Prague 1 (Zahraniční časopisy). Newstands are indentified by the letters PNS (for *Poštovní Novinová Služba,* post news service).

Do you have any English-language newspapers?	**Máte nějaké noviny v ancličtině?**

P **PHOTOGRAPHY.** Film is relatively expensive, and so is speedy processing. Most of the film available is locally made Foma and East German Orwo.

Don't take pictures where a sign indicates photography is prohibited.

I'd like some film for this camera.	**Prosím film do tohoto aparátu.**
colour print/colour slides	**barevné kopie/barevné diapozitivy**
May I take a picture?	**Smím fotografovat?**

POLICE *(policie).* The police wear military-style olive-drab uniforms, but with white blouses in summer. Police patrol cars are yellow and white with the letters VB (for *Veřejná Bezpečnost,* public security) on either side.

Police headquarters is at Konviktská 14, Staré Město, Prague 1.

The police emergency telephone number is 158.

Where's the nearest police station?	**Kde je nejbližší oddělení Veřejné bezpečnosti?**

PUBLIC HOLIDAYS

January 1	*Nový rok*	New Year's Day
May 1	*Svátek práce*	May Day
May 9	*Vítězství nad fašismem*	Victory over Fascism
July 5	*Slovanští věrozvěsti sv. Cyril a Metoděj*	Slavic Missionaries St. Cyril and St. Methodius
October 28	*První československá republika*	First Czechoslovak Republic
December 24	*Štědrý den*	Christmas Eve
December 25-26	*Svátek vánoční*	Christmas/ Boxing Day
Movable date:	*Velikonoční pondělí*	Easter Monday

Are you open tomorrow?	**Máte zítra otevřeno?**

R **RADIO and TV** *(rozhlas; televize).* Prague has three radio stations, one of which (Radio Inter) has five-minute news broadcasts in English, French, German and Russian every hour, on the hour. There are three television channels, broadcasting most programmes in colour.

Channel 1 is on the air across the country from early morning to around midnight; Channel 2 features regional programmes. Foreign films are almost always dubbed rather than subtitled. Channel 3 broadcasts a review of Satellite programmes in their original languages from 4 p.m. to 11 p.m.

News in English from the BBC or Voice of America can be picked up on short-wave transistor radios.

RELIGIOUS SERVICES. As you'll soon discover from the proliferation of churches, Prague is a mainly Catholic city. A notice posted at the main entrance gives the times of masses. There are no services in foreign languages.

Some of Prague's historic synagogues are open for services, as well.

TIME DIFFERENCES. Czechoslovakia follows Central European Time (GMT + 1). From late March until late September clocks are put ahead one hour (GMT + 2).

Summer time chart:

Los Angeles	New York	London	**Prague**	Sydney	Auckland
3 a.m.	6 a.m.	11 a.m.	**noon**	8 p.m.	10 p.m.

TIPPING. For ideological reasons the subject can be controversial. Nonetheless, most workers who deal with tourists accept and appreciate tips. The chart below will give you some guidelines.

Hotel doorman for taxi	10 Kčs
Hotel porter, per bag	5 Kčs
Hotel maid, per week	30 Kčs
Lavatory attendant	1 Kčs
Cloakroom (hatcheck) attendant	2 Kčs
Waiter	10%
Taxi driver	10%
Hairdresser/Barber	10%

| Tour guide | 50 Kčs |
| Theatre usher | 1–2 Kčs (if buying programme) |

Keep the change.   **Ponechte si drobné.**

TOILETS. Your best bet is to seek out the conveniences in a hotel or restaurant or Metro (underground/subway) station. Toilets are often signposted in the English manner, "WC". Men's facilites may be marked "Muži" or "Páni", and women's "Ženy" or "Dámy" or by picture-signs.

Where are the toilets?   **Kde jsou toalety?**

TOURIST INFORMATION OFFICES. For general and specific information and tourist brochures about Czechoslovakia, consult Čedok, the country's oldest and largest travel agency. Some Čedok addresses abroad:

North America   10 East 40th Street, New York, N.Y. 10016; tel. (212) 689-9720.
United Kingdom   17–18, Old Bond Street, London W1X 3DA; tel. (01) 629-6058/9.

In Prague, there are Foreign Travel Division offices of Čedok at:
Na příkopě 18, Prague 1; tel. 21 27 111
Bílkova 6, Prague 1; tel. 23 18 255
Wenceslas Square 24; tel. 23 56 356

Or look for the Prague Information Service centres:
Na příkopě 20, Prague 1; tel. 54 44 44
Hradčanská Metro station; tel. 32 29 17.

Where's the tourist office?   **Kde je cestovní kancelář?**

TRANSPORT

Metro (underground or subway). Prague's showcase Metro system is clean, bright, fast and cheap. There are even signboards that tell you how much time has elapsed since the last train departed. Even if you don't need the Metro for getting around, it's worth taking a ride for the experience. The system runs from 5 a.m. to midnight.

Metro stations are clearly marked by an "M" symbol, part of an arrow design pointing downwards. Before you enter, buy a ticket from one of the machines in the entrance hall. The investment entitles you to an underground ride of any distance, including free transfers among the three Metro lines (within an hour and a half). You can also buy a pass valid for 24 hours on all forms of public transport in Prague. Anyone caught without a valid ticket or pass can be fined.

Maps of the Metro system are posted in the stations and inside the trains. Recorded announcements en route identify the stops.

Trams *(tramvay* or *elektrika)*. A comprehensive tram (streetcar) network provides cheap surface transport throughout the city and into the outskirts. At each tram stop a chart lists the routes and timetables (though some of the posted schedules seem purely theoretical). Tram tickets are sold at newsstands or from coin-operated machines at stations. There are no conductors; when you board, validate your ticket in the machine near the door. Free transfers are not given; you must use a new ticket for each leg of your trip. Some trams run all night, though at long intervals.

Buses *(autobus)*. Since tram lines efficiently cover the metropolitan area, buses are generally assigned to longer distances. The itineraries are posted at bus stops. There are some night bus routes. On local lines a bus rider needs the same ticket as Metro or tram passengers; punch it yourself when you board.

Inter-city bus routes link all the main towns. For information on long-distance schedules, telephone 22 14 45, 22 86 42 or 22 14 40.

Taxis. The best place to find a taxi is at a taxi rank, for example outside hotels, department stores and railway stations. Radio taxis can be booked by telephone: 20 39 41 or 20 29 51. The meter indicates the fare, but there may be extra charges, for instance for baggage or for leaving the city limits.

Trains. An extensive rail network with first- and second-class service covers the entire country. Trains are generally comfortable but are not always punctual or very clean. Since they tend to get crowded, it's advisable to book in advance. Note that the big, modernized Main Station (Praha-Hlavní nádraží) is more convenient than Masaryk Station (Masarykovo nadraží), formerly known as Central Station. For information on train connections, telephone 26 49 30 or 23 64 441.

I'd like a ticket to…	**Prosím jízdenku do…**
single (one-way)/return	**jednoduchou/zpáteční**
Will you tell me where to get off?	**Prosím, povíte mi kde mám vystoupit?**

WATER. It's perfectly safe to drink water from the tap anywhere in Prague. Or try some wholesome Czechoslovakian mineral water, bottled at well-known spas.

I'd like a bottle of mineral water.	**Prosím láhev minerálky.**
fizzy (carbonated)/still	**sodovku minerálku/přírodní minerálku**

SOME USEFUL EXPRESSIONS

yes/no	**ano/ne**
please/thank you	**prosím/děkuji**
excuse me/you're welcome	**promiňte/poslužte si**
where/when/how	**kde (kam)/kdy/jak**
how long/how far	**jak dlouho/jak daleko**
yesterday/today/tomorrow	**včera/dnes/zítra**
day/week/month/year	**den/týden/měsíc/rok**
left/right	**levý/pravý (vlevo/vpravo)**
up/down	**nahoru/dolů (nahoře/dole)**
good/bad	**dobrý/špatný**
big/small	**velký/malý**
cheap/expensive	**levný/drahý**
old/new	**starý/nový**
old/young	**starý/mladý**
hot/cold	**horký/studený**
open/closed	**otevřeno/zavřeno**
free (vacant)/occupied	**volný/obsazený**
near/far	**blízko/daleko**
early/late	**brzy/pozdě**
Waiter/Waitress, please.	**Pane/Paní vrchní, prosím.**
I'd like…	**Chtěl bych… (Prosím…)**
How much is that?	**Co to stojí?**
Monday/Tuesday/Wednesday	**pondělí/úterý/středa**
Thurday/Friday	**čtvrtek/pátek**
Saturday/Sunday	**sobota/neděle**

Index

An asterix (*) next to a page number indicates a map reference. Where there is more than one set of page references, the one in bold type refers to the main entry. For the index to Practical Information, see inside front cover.

039/104 RP